MAKING SENSE OF RELIGION

IN AMERICA'S PUBLIC SCHOOLS

MOST FREQUENTLY ASKED
PUBLIC SCHOOL QUESTIONS ABOUT RELIGION
AS IT RELATES TO
STUDENT RIGHTS, TEACHER RIGHTS,
CURRICULUM, AND OUTREACH

Atty. David C. Gibbs III
with Atty. Barbara J. Weller

A Publication of

The National Center for Life and Liberty

P.O. Box 12827
St. Petersburg, FL 33733-2827

www.NCLL.org

Published by The National Center for Life and Liberty,
P.O. Box 12827, St. Petersburg, FL 33733-2827

www.NCLL.org

Printed in the United States of America

MAKING SENSE OF RELIGION IN AMERICA'S PUBLIC SCHOOLS

Most Frequently Asked Public School Questions about Religion as It Relates to Student Rights, Teacher Rights, Curriculum, And Outreach

INTRODUCTION 1

CONCERNING STUDENTS 5

May students still pray in public school? 6

May students bring their Bibles to school and read them in school? 8

May students distribute tracts in public school? 9

May students include religion in school assignments? 11

May students be excused from school for religious holidays and/or activities? 14

May a student be excused from participation in classroom activities that are religiously objectionable? 15

Must a student participate in religiously objectionable holiday activities in school? 16

May a student wear religious apparel in school, such as a T-shirt with a religious slogan? 18

May students organize Bible clubs at school 19

May students use notebooks, pencils, and other material with religious logos or sayings, including Bible verses? 22

May students engage in group religious activities such as See You at the Pole? 23

May a student mention religion in a graduation speech? 23

Must students be permitted to wear modest dress in gym class if their religion requires it? 24

May students be permitted to use religious material in a school talent show? 25

May students talk about religion in class discussions? 26

Key Cases Supporting Student Rights

Student Free Speech 27

Religious Expression 31

Official School-Sponsored Religious Speech 33

Student Religious Speech 35

Distribution of Religious Materials 38

Student Assignments 44

Religious Accommodations and Opt Out Rights 46

Clothing with Religious Messages 48

Equal Access Clubs 50

See You at the Pole 53

Letters and Guidelines

Letter from U.S. Department of Education Concerning Students' Rights to Religious Expression in Public Schools 54

Presidential Guidelines on Religious Expression in Public Schools (Revised May 1998) 59

Secretary's Letter on Constitutionally Protected Prayer in Public Elementary and Secondary Schools 63

Guidance on Constitutionally Protected Prayer in Public Elementary and Secondary Schools 64

Equal Access Act (20 U.S.C. §4071) 75

Concerning Teachers, School Staff, and Officials

What free speech and free exercise rights do teachers still retain in public schools? 80

May teachers communicate with other school personnel about religion either in conversations or in writing? 80

May teachers include religious references in correspondence with parents of students? 81

May teachers post inspirational messages from the Bible on faculty-only bulletin boards? 81

May teachers hold faculty Bible studies or prayer groups in public schools? 82

May teachers keep a personal Bible or other religious material on their desk? 83

May teachers wear religious clothing or jewelry in the classroom? 83

May teachers who object to political or anti-religious positions taken by teachers' unions withhold that portion of union dues? 84

May teachers pray privately with students outside of class? 84

May teachers give their personal viewpoint in answer to a student's questions about religion? 85

May teachers interact with students regarding religion while away from the school campus? 86

May teachers talk about personal religious viewpoints in the classroom? 87

May teachers permit students to discuss religion in the classroom? 89

May teachers participate in student Bible clubs? 90

May teachers participate in student-initiated and student-led prayer activities such as "See You At the Pole"? 91

May coaches lead sports teams in prayer before games? 91

May a school bus driver, cafeteria worker, janitor or secretary talk to students about religion or pray with them? 92

KEY CASES IMPACTING RIGHTS OF TEACHERS IN PUBLIC SCHOOLS

Teacher Interaction with Other School Personnel 93

Teachers' Unions 94

Religious Speech by Teachers in the Classroom 95

Religious Speech by Coaches 99

Teacher Participation in Student Religious Activities 100

Guidelines on Religious Exercise and Religious Expression in the Federal Workplace 101

CONCERNING CURRICULUM

Has the Supreme Court prohibited all prayer and Bible reading in public schools? 119

May the Bible be taught as part of the academic curriculum? 121

Where may the Bible be included in a public school's academic curriculum? 122

What constitutes objective, neutral, and academic classroom teaching about religion? 123

May a public school teach an elective course in world religions? 126

How should a public school select teachers for elective Bible or religion courses? 126

How does instruction in the Bible fit into elementary education? 127

How can the Bible be included in a literature course? 127

How can the Bible be included in a history course? 130

May teaching about religious holidays be included in the public school curriculum? 131

What should a teacher do if specifically told by superiors not to teach a particular religious concept or holiday in the classroom? 133

May a teacher include religious music in music classes or choral programs? 134

May a teacher display religious artwork on schoolroom walls? 136

May teachers permit students to choose religious material to fulfill assignments or reading requirements? 137

Must a school permit students to opt out of a religiously objectionable class or assignment? 138

May a voluntary reading program include religious books? 140

May religious books be included in the school library or in a teacher's classroom library? 142

May courses stressing values and morals be included in the school curriculum? 142

May teachers teach creation in biology classes that study evolution? 143

May a public school open the school day with a "moment of silence" that includes the opportunity for individual student prayer? 145

What religious expression is appropriate for graduation exercises? 146

CASES THAT PERMIT TEACHING ABOUT RELIGION AND THE BIBLE IN PUBLIC SCHOOLS 149

Art, Music, and Holidays 151

How to Teach the Bible 155

Prohibiting Religion in Public Schools 160

Opt Out Policies 162

Issues of Creation/Evolution 165

Moment of Silence 167

Graduation Prayer 170

Other School Prayer Activities 174

Sioux Falls School District Religion Policy 177

Duval County Graduation Messasge Guidelines 180

CONCERNING OUTSIDE COMMUNITY VOLUNTEERS 181

What may religious volunteers do to assist an Equal Access Bible Club? 183

What is a Released Time program? 184

How may churches or other community sponsors implement a Released Time program? 184

How may parents, students and/or community sponsors obtain permission from the school board to establish a Released Time program? 186

Who determines what is taught in the Released Time program? 187

May outside groups sponsor after-school Bible clubs for students on school property? 188

May churches rent school facilities for worship services? 188

Where may outside sponsors conduct baccalaureate services? 189

May Gideons distribute Bibles in public schools? 190

May soulwinners distribute tracts and talk to students on sidewalks that abut school property? 191

May pastors visit with students during lunch periods? 192

May public school counseling programs include pastors? 192

May a school distribute notices in class for outside religious activities available to students? 193

Key Cases Regarding Volunteers

Released Time Programs 195

Use of Public Schools by Outside Groups 198

Private Baccalaureate Services 200

Distribution of Religious Materials 201

Witnessing in Public Forum Areas Around Public Schools 203

Involvement of Religious Leaders in School Programs 205

Notice Distribution for Religious Programs 206

INTRODUCTION

In 1947, the United States Supreme Court took a sharp left turn in its interpretation of the Establishment Clause of the First Amendment to the United States Constitution as it was applied to public schools in America. Since then, students, teachers, school officials, parents, and local religious leaders have been struggling to understand the parameters of the Establishment Clause as it relates to religious expression in public schools. This resource is intended to help individuals understand their rights to exercise their faith in the public school arena.

The decision of the United States Supreme Court in the case of *Everson v. Board of Education*, 330 U.S. 1 (1947), was the first time the United States Supreme Court held that the Establishment Clause restrained individual states and all other governmental entities from establishing or officially sponsoring religion. When Congress enacted the Bill of Rights in 1789, the Establishment Clause was intended to restrain only the conduct of the federal government. At that point in our nation's history, states were left to establish a state religion if they wished. Therefore, since public schools were creatures of state and local governments, local governing bodies, such as school boards, could include the dominant religious beliefs of the community in the local school curriculum.

In the *Everson* case, the Court upheld a New Jersey statute permitting the state to reimburse Catholic parents for the expense of busing their children to and from parochial schools. However, in doing so, the Court ruled for the first time that the Establishment Clause prohibited all governmental entities, not just the federal government, from establishing religion. Many of the early American colonies had established dominant religious institutions. Although these state churches had fallen out of favor over time, the *Everson* decision constitutionally required all other governmental bodies to also abandon the practice. It was primarily this extension of the Establishment Clause to all governmental entities, including public schools, that became the source of today's controversies regarding prayer and religious education in taxpayer-supported schools.

The *Everson* Court held that New Jersey's transportation legislation did no more than provide a general program to help parents, regardless of their religion, to safely and efficiently transport their children to school. Therefore, the Court said, this law did not breach the "high and impregnable" wall of separation between church and state. The Everson decision was the first time the United States Supreme Court imposed Thomas Jefferson's "wall of separation" word picture as a governing principle in America's constitutional law.

The "wall of separation" was a phrase used by President Thomas Jefferson in a letter he wrote to the Danbury Baptist Convention in 1801. In response to a letter from the Convention expressing concern that the Constitution permitted the federal government to interfere in matters of religion, Jefferson assured this Connecticut church body that it had no need to fear intervention from the federal government because a "wall of separation" had been constitutionally erected between church and state.

The Court's majority decision in the Everson case, written by Justice Hugo Black, held that it was constitutional for New Jersey public school districts to transport Catholic school students to their parochial schools, but then went on to state:

> The First Amendment has erected a wall of separation between church and state. That wall must be kept high and impregnable. We could not approve the slightest breach. New Jersey has not breached it here.

This unprecedented conclusion followed a strong statement by the Court several pages earlier that specifically spelled out what the "high and impregnable" wall implied:

> Neither a state nor the Federal Government can set up a church. Neither can pass laws which aid one religion, aid all religions, or prefer one religion over another. . . . No tax in any amount, large or small, can be levied to support any religious activities or institutions, whatever they may be called, or whatever form they may adopt to teach or practice religion.

The *Everson* Court's application of the Establishment Clause to state and local governments, including school boards, and its elevation of Thomas Jefferson's "wall of separation" comment to a constitutional principle continue even today to provide the legal bases for the exclusion of prayer and other official religious activities from public schools even against the wishes of the electorate and the parents.

Under current judicial interpretations of the Establishment Clause, a democratically elected school board may not recognize or accommodate the religious viewpoints of a majority of the school population into the school's curriculum even if minority students are not required to participate in or to agree with the religious exercises (such as prayer at graduation or before football games). However, one court has ruled that religious students were required to attend homosexuality diversity training classes in school even if those classes violated their religious beliefs and the values being taught to them by their parents. Why? Because the students were not required to agree with the presentation. This is clearly a double standard being imposed upon students by our courts. Such modern court decisions undermine parental rights and the democratic process by which public schools were intended to operate under the control of democratically elected school boards that reflect the values of each school community.

While it does not appear that making religion an outlaw in public schools was the intent of the founders, nor was it the practice in America before 1947, the *Everson* decision set the stage for other challenges to religious practices in public schools. Daily prayer and Bible reading were challenged and dismissed from public schools in the early 1960s. Other forms of official religious expression became legally unwelcome in public schools with the elimination of graduation prayers in 1992 and prayers before football games in 2000. All religious limitations in public schools are based on the 1947 Court-imposed interpretation of the Establishment Clause as requiring a complete "separation of church and state" in all federal, state, and local governments. Interestingly, however, some courts continue to permit the teaching of non-Christian religions in public schools under the guise that such instruction is "cultural" and not religious." This, too, is a double standard being imposed by modern courts on our nation's public schools.

There is good news, however. Despite the Establishment Clause's limitation on official religious expression in public schools, the First Amendment's Free Speech and Free Exercise Clauses continue to protect most student religious speech in public schools. Most courts also adopt a reasonable approach to religious instruction in public schools. Even while the Establishment Clause, since the mid-Twentieth Century, has prohibited devotional and proselytizing religious speech by public school teachers and other school officials, teachers may still teach about religion in public schools if such teaching is objective, neutral, and academic. Court decisions in the last half century have also continued to protect at least some religious outreach activities in public schools by community religious leaders.

This resource is intended to assist families, students, teachers, school officials and community leaders to sort through the current legal maze of religious expression in America's public schools. We want to encourage the free exercise of every available legal right of speech and religious expression in order to be faithful to the intent of America's founders and to the successful education of today's public school students.

CONCERNING STUDENTS

A public school may not entirely prohibit religious activities by students. The Free Speech and Free Exercise Clauses of the First Amendment to the United States Constitution protect most student religious speech in public school. While teachers are limited in their devotional and proselytizing religious interaction with students by the First Amendment Establishment Clause, students have a great deal of spontaneous or unofficial religious liberty in public schools, even in today's separationist and anti-Christian legal and educational climate. Since government schools permit students to speak with each other and to exchange viewpoints on many topics, the government must also permit students to engage in religious speech and to share their religious viewpoints in school, so long as these activities are not "disruptive" to the educational climate---an exception that in some cases allows modern courts to swallow the rule. A public school could require students to be completely silent during the school day; however, since public schools have not chosen to do that, free speech rights must apply equally to all students. Religious students may not be singled out for prohibitions when others are permitted to speak. Various courts have said that free speech includes religious speech, even including activities such as prayer, Bible reading and tract distribution.

> *Students have a great deal of spontaneous or unofficial religious liberty in public schools.*

In order to resolve growing confusion concerning students' free speech rights with regard to religion, President Bill Clinton instructed then-Secretary of Education Richard Riley in 1995 to provide every public school district in the United States with a statement of principles addressing the extent to which religious expression and activity are legally permitted in public schools. These guiding principles, known as the *Presidential Guidelines on Student Expression in Public Schools*, were updated in 1998 to their current form. In addition, on February 7, 2003, President George W. Bush's Education Secretary, Rod Paige, issued an update on student religious rights in public schools as part of the implementation of the *No Child Left Be-*

hind Act of 2001. The *Secretary's Letter on Constitutionally Protected Prayer* reaffirms that the First Amendment protects the following student religious activities:

- Voluntary individual or group prayer before meals, tests, and at other times when such activity will not disrupt classroom instruction;
- Voluntary student Bible reading during non-instructional periods;
- Religious conversations with classmates during non-instructional periods. Students may even attempt to persuade their peers concerning religious topics as long as such attempts at persuasion do not constitute harassment or actually disrupt the educational environment;
- "See-you-at-the-pole" gatherings;
- Distribution of religious literature;
- Wearing clothing or apparel with religious messages to the same extent as secular messages are allowed; and
- Incorporating religious views and beliefs in homework, artwork, and other written and oral assignments.

The two government publications, the *Presidential Guidelines on Student Expression in Public School* and the *Secretary's Letter on Constitutionally Protected Prayer*, are both included in full at the end of this section. School officials, parents, students, and teachers should consult these federal documents as authoritative when questions arise regarding the religious rights of students in public schools.

The following questions are commonly asked by public school students.

May students still pray in public school?

Prayer that is genuinely student initiated—religious speech without any oversight or supervision from school officials—is still permitted in public schools. The only prayer that courts have banned in public schools is officially sponsored prayer or student prayer that is either directed or encouraged by teachers or other school officials.

The First Amendment Establishment Clause (which courts since the mid-Twentieth Century have interpreted by using "the doctrine of the separation of church and state") does not prohibit a student's personal expression of prayer in school. In fact, the First Amendment protects free speech and free exercise rights for students, even in public school.

'The doctrine of the separation of church and state" does not prohibit a student's personal expression of prayer in school.

A student may pray silently or quietly out loud, alone or in a group, but may not disturb, harass or disrupt other students. As long as the prayer is spontaneous and is not encouraged by a teacher or by school policy, the prayer is permitted. Students may say grace before lunch at school, and they may pray before tests to the same extent that they may engage in comparable secular non-disruptive activities. For instance, while one student or several students sitting together could pray out loud before lunch, they would not be permitted to pray loudly enough to be heard by everyone throughout the cafeteria. Such actions would be prohibited because they are disruptive and because they would involve a "captive audience" of other students. Nevertheless, students are free to quietly pray aloud alone or in groups. If the speech level is reasonable, there is no constitutional foul, even if a student sitting at the next table is able to overhear a quiet prayer.

Students may say grace before lunch at school and they may pray before tests.

Students are still permitted to pray spontaneously alone or in groups at school. Far too many little children have been traumatized when told they may not bow their heads and silently or quietly say grace before eating their lunch or Kindergarten snack. This is an outrageous misinterpretation of the "separation of church and state" doctrine by school officials and it undermines the religious instruction of the family and church.

The United States Supreme Court has said that student prayer before football games violates the Constitution's Establishment Clause; however, in that case, an official school policy encouraged the prayer and the school also provided a public address system for the prayer. Football players may still spontaneously gather mid-field on their own initiative for a group prayer before a game as long as no school officials are involved and the prayer is voluntary. These are constitutional rights of free expression personal to the student and they are still protected by the Free Speech and Free Exercise Clauses of the First Amendment.

May students bring their Bibles to school and read them in school?

Since students may bring books to school that are not part of the school curriculum to read during study hall or free-reading times, the government school may not prohibit a book such as the Bible merely because it is religious. Both carrying a Bible and reading it in school are constitutional free speech rights routinely protected for public school students by courts. Unofficial student religious speech has nothing whatsoever to do with the Establishment Clause or with the modern legal doctrine of "separation of church and state."

Only a teacher or other school official is capable of violating the Establishment Clause. A student is not legally capable of violating the Establishment Clause because the Establishment Clause does not apply to students, but only to school or other government officials. Public school students are consumers of a government program. They are not government agents, as teachers and other school officials are. Therefore, a student may engage in private religious speech and religious activity, such as carrying a Bible or reading it during free time in school (even in the classroom at appropriate reading times). This area of the law has been well settled for decades.

Both carrying a Bible and reading it in school are constitutionally protected free speech.

There is no doubt that a student's constitutionally protected free speech and free exercise of religion rights would be violated if the student were not permitted to bring a Bible to school or to read it at appropriate times in school. Schools are not religion-free zones. In fact, students may also spontaneously gather in groups over lunch or during other appropriate free time to study and discuss the Bible together. This free speech right is equivalent to the right students have to gather in groups over lunch or in the hallway to discuss a previous night's TV program or some other topic of mutual interest. As long as such activities do not disrupt the academic work of the school program, they are legally permitted forms of free speech.

May students distribute tracts in public school?

Christian students are sometimes challenged by school officials when they attempt to distribute Christian literature or Gospel tracts to other students. Tract distribution by students outside the classroom without harassment and at appropriate time does not violate the Establishment Clause, but is a protected right of free speech. Free speech includes both the spoken and the printed word. Since students are not agents or employees of the government school system, it is impossible for a student to violate the Establishment Clause by giving a tract to another student, without harassment and at an appropriate non-academic time.

Schools are not religion-free zones.

Students have the same right to distribute religious literature to their schoolmates as they do to distribute other written material that is unrelated to the official school curriculum or activities. Schools may impose the same reasonable time, place, and manner regulations on the distribution of religious literature as they do on non-school-related literature generally, but they may not single out religious literature for special regulation or prohibition. A tract is no different from a note passed to a classmate about meeting for shopping after school. Since note passing is generally prohibited in the classroom, tract distribution may also be prohibited in the classroom. A teacher may legitimately close the classroom for everything except curriculum-related speech and activities, but may not single out only student religious speech for prohibition.

The legal standard for student speech is that the school may not impose different rules for written religious material (such as a tract) than it does for secular written material (such as a note or birthday party invitation). All are student free speech activities that are protected when carried out in appropriate situations during the school day. If a school wanted to stop student-to-student tract distribution in school, it would be required to stop all student speech, whether oral or written. Neutral time, place, and manner regulations are permitted to control student speech in general, but all speech must be regulated in the same manner. There can be no special rules for student-to-student religious speech than for other speech.

Tract distribution by students outside the classroom does not violate the Establishment Clause.

As with all speech in school, it is important to remember that it would be harassment to force another student to take a tract or to continue to offer tracts to other students when they have previously indicated that the tract (or religious speech in general) is not welcome.

Students should generally follow the following four rules to make sure that tract distribution is not disruptive:

1. Only distribute tracts outside of the classroom (distribution may not interfere with academics).

2. Never leave tracts unattended—in bathrooms or on benches, for instance.

3. Never force other students to take the tracts. Offer one for them to take if they want to. If students decline or indicate they do not wish to be approached again, the tract distributor should leave those students alone. It would be considered harassment for a student to force another student to take a tract, or to persist in witnessing after other students indicate they are unwilling to receive the communication. The same principles should also be applied by school officials to secular

students who harass Christians in school.

4. Never distribute tracts that denigrate other religions. Civility of speech is required in public schools, and denigrating another student's religion is considered uncivil conduct that could be prohibited, no matter what the subject matter. Students should only distribute positive tracts and none with scary pictures of demons, etc.—particularly for the elementary school environment.

May students include religion in school assignments?

When teachers give their students a choice of subject matter for an assignment, the students may express their own beliefs about religion in the form of homework, artwork, or other written and oral assignments, as long as the assignment otherwise meets the teacher's academic objectives and requirements. Teachers must then judge homework and classroom work containing religious expression by using the same ordinary academic standards they would apply to non-religious expression.

The Supreme Court has stated that if a government school prohibits religious speech or activities, it would be demonstrating not neutrality, but an unconstitutional hostility toward religion. The Establishment Clause does not permit the government, including public schools, to treat religion and those who practice it differently or in any negative way that would subject the religious student to unique disabilities.

> *If a government school prohibits religious speech or activities, it would be demonstrating not neutrality but an unconstitutional hostility toward religion.*

Students may give speeches, choose show-and-tell displays, present talent show selections, or do artwork using religious themes as long as the teacher has given the student a choice in topic selection and the student is careful to follow other general assignment instructions. Generally, school officials may only censor student speech for obscenity, promoting drugs, or for general lack of civility. Therefore, any time students are given a choice of subject matter in an assignment; a religious choice must be permitted, however, the choice should not be devotional or proselytizing. Some examples include the following: choosing to read a Christian book when other students are permitted to choose books for making a report, choosing a religious show-and-tell item, choosing a religious topic for a speech, choosing a religious topic for a writing assignment, or choosing a religious theme for an art project or talent show presentation. Religious artwork may be displayed alongside secular artwork where it is obvious that the choice of subject matter was the student's choice. To prohibit such choices would be viewpoint discrimination in violation of the First Amendment rights of free speech and would demonstrate an unconstitutional hostility toward religion and toward religious students.

Students may write book reports or English themes or do discretionary assignments about religious subjects. However, such reports must closely follow all academic assignment instructions because a teacher may reject a religious assignment when it is not considered appropriate for that particular pedagogical exercise. For example, one teacher legally refused to allow a child to show a videotape of herself singing a Christian song because the purpose of the class assignment had been to increase the students' communication skills by requiring a "live" classroom presentation by the student on a subject of the student's choosing.

> *Any time students are given a choice of subject matter in an assignment, a religious choice must be permitted.*

When the choice to use a religious topic is the student's and not the teacher's, there is no violation of the Establishment Clause, since students, as consumers rather than providers of government services, are not able to violate the Establishment Clause. Only teachers or other school officials are able to violate the Establishment Clause. The teacher can explain to the rest of the class that the topic choice is the student's and that the viewpoint expressed is that of the student. Therefore, speeches with non-devotional and non-proselytizing religious content may be given in class to other students and student artwork with a religious theme may be hung in a classroom, as long as it is clear to the hearer or to the observer that the religious choice and viewpoint was the student's. Students who would not want to hear a religious presentation that would violate their own religious beliefs could be excused from the classroom for the duration of the presentation upon a written request from the student's parents.

In most cases where courts have not supported a student's right to choose a religious topic for an assignment, the courts have determined that the student did not meet the teacher's pedagogical requirements or that the student's religious choice appeared to have official school endorsement. Where the assignment otherwise meets the teacher's academic requirements and the use of the assignment does not appear to have official school endorsement, there is no constitutional violation in such individual student choices. If a teacher does not wish to permit a student to make a religious choice in completing an assignment, the teacher should not permit any of the students to have a free choice in the assignment topic.

The federal government has said that public schools must treat religion with fairness and respect and must vigorously protect student religious expression, as well as the religious consciences of all students. This directive pertains to religious speech both inside and outside the classroom. Many teachers would find it very interesting, for instance, to have a Muslim student explain his beliefs and customs in a classroom speech. That same teacher may not then prohibit a Christian student from also explaining his Christian beliefs and practices. Insofar as Islam is a cultural as well as a religious topic, the same is also true of Christianity; and the two should be treated exactly alike in school. The teacher should assume that hearing about the beliefs and customs of a Christian student is no more proselytizing or inappropriate than hearing about the beliefs and customs of a Muslim student. Both can have educational value for the rest of the class and both can be used by the teacher to encourage a respect for all viewpoints, including those with which the student disagrees. The American experiment encourages persuasive and open debate about all topics.

May students be excused from school for religious holidays and/or activities?

Schools should excuse students for religious holidays and activities as part of the religious accommodation schools are required to provide for students. This accommodation may include excusing a child for a religious holiday, such as Good Friday, if the school is not already closed. It might also include excusing a child from class in order to fulfill religious requirements—such as prayers during Ramadan for Muslim students.

Policies in this area are set by local school boards elected by the citizens. Most schools have written policies governing religious excusals. The parent should ask about the school's policy and follow the requirements of the policy in requesting a religious excusal for the child. Parents should remain alert to make certain that schools are not permitting one group, such as Muslims, to be excused for religious activities if other students, such as Christians or Jews, are not granted similar permission to fulfill their religious duties. A school may not engage in unequal treatment of religious students in violation of the Fourteenth Amendment, which requires equal treatment for all. School board policies sometimes limit excusals to religious holidays; however, a school board policy may also permit excusals for other religious activities, perhaps limited to two or three days per year.

One common question involves religious excusals for situations involving sports teams or school choirs where the group might hold practices or games at a time that conflicts with a religious activity, such as Wednesday night church services. This becomes a more difficult problem with respect to extracurricular activities. School board policies should take into account family time and time for religious duties. However, a school may be dealing with students who have many differing religious expressions and activities. One student might need to be absent every Wednesday night, another every Friday night, depending upon their particular religious observances. While the school board and individual teachers should make every effort to accommodate religious students, it may be difficult for a group such as a chorus or sports team to accommodate regular absences for religious observances for every group, since those observances would often conflict. A sports team generally also involves other schools in its competition schedule. Schools are not required to make religious accommodations that are unreasonable in light of the total program.

May a student be excused from participation in classroom activities that are religiously objectionable?

Schools are generally required to accommodate the religious beliefs of their students. Students and parents may have religious objections to certain assignments, classes, or activities in public school. Parents have a free exercise claim, in many cases, to prevent their children from being taught material that would negatively impact or burden their own sincerely held religious beliefs. If the school does not have a compelling reason for requiring every child to participate in a particular activity, class or assignment, the school must allow the student to "opt out" of the activity, class or assignment at the request of the parent.

School boards enjoy substantial discretion to develop "opt out" policies for excusing individual students from lessons or activities that are objectionable on religious grounds and that violate the student's sincerely held religious beliefs. Generally, this right to opt out is exercised by the parent giving written notice to the teacher, and in some cases, also to the principal, explaining the religious objection and requesting that the student be permitted to engage in a substitute activity or be excused from the classroom during the objectionable class activity. The teacher is prohibited from denigrating the student's actions in leaving the classroom or in engaging in a comparable activity. The teacher is also prohibited from punishing the student—by lowering a grade for instance—for exercising these religious rights.

The opt out process is often made considerably smoother if the parent is able to suggest an alternative subject or activity to the teacher that would be acceptable. Instead of reading Harry Potter books, for example, the student could read a comparable fantasy series such as the Chronicles of Narnia by C.S. Lewis. A teacher is often more inclined to facilitate the opt out request when the parent provides an acceptable alternative assignment possibility along with the opt out request.

Some parents opt out their children from viewing inappropriate films in school. If the family's religious beliefs do not permit the child to view an objectionable film, the teacher should assign an alternative activity and permit the student to leave the classroom and work in the library or other reasonable location while the film is shown. The child should never be required to stand outside in the hall, as though being punished, while the objectionable classroom activity is ongoing.

If there is a large group of parents interested in this issue, the group, rather than just individual parents, should approach the school board to request an appropriate policy for student films or reading assignments. Finally, if a large group of students in a class request to opt out from a particularly offensive activity, such as viewing a profane film, the group may be able to influence the teacher to change the assignment or activity. If more students are in the library reading other books than are in the classroom working on the original assignment, it is unlikely the teacher would continue the offensive assignment.

Must a student participate in religiously objectionable holiday activities in school?

There are two ways to approach religiously objectionable holiday activities in public schools. One option is to approach the school board and request that the offensive holiday be eliminated from the school curriculum. The school board is elected by the community and is legally expected to represent the perspective of the majority of the community in such matters. The more people in a school district who object to celebrating a particular holiday and can approach the school board in a unified manner, the more likely it is that the school board would listen and act on the objection.

The school board should be asked to consider eliminating the offensive activity or substituting a celebration that is neutral in character, such as a "Fall Festival" instead of "Halloween." This is a good strategy—particularly if Christians who oppose the offensive celebrations are in the majority in the community, or at least are in the majority on the elected school board. This area is discretionary with the school board as are many other curriculum matters.

Christians should also consider their political option of electing a school board that supports the community viewpoint on the religiously offensive holiday activities. A school board that is sensitive to such religious issues can be extremely helpful in setting policies that are religion friendly. It is vitally important for the care and education of school children for parents to be concerned about who serves on the local school board.

If the school board does not agree to drop the offensive holiday activities, the best that can be done is for individual parents to opt their children out of participation. The child could be permitted to stay home on the day of the activity with no penalty or could be given other activities to substitute for the objectionable holiday-related activities. If the teacher is not amenable to the opt out and a substitute assignment, the parent should go to the principal, superintendent, and school board, in that order, to protect the child's right to the free exercise of religion in school.

This option for dealing with holiday activities that offend religious beliefs is based on the rights of children and parents to have their religious beliefs accommodated by the school. Every professional classroom teacher should be concerned not to offend the religious beliefs of any child in her classroom—whether Christian, Muslim, or any other religion. Professional, conscientious teachers should educate themselves ahead of time about the religious sensitivities of every child and parent represented in the classroom; and attempt to avoid problems before they arise.

This situation must also be monitored in the reverse as many school boards are currently attempting to eliminate holidays such as Christmas on the grounds that they are "offensive" to some students. In this situation, the majority of families should make clear to the school board that holidays such as Christmas and Easter should not be eliminated from the school calendar. Those few students who might find this religious holiday offensive may opt out of participation in the activities involved. The school board should be concerned to represent the majority of its constituents, while continuing to respect the minority of students who do not share the views of the majority.

May a student wear religious apparel in school, such as a T-shirt with a religious slogan?

It would be religious discrimination for a government school to generally permit students to wear clothing (such as T-shirts or sweatshirts) with slogans or logos, but then to discipline a student for wearing clothing with a religious or pro-life slogan or logo. Wearing message clothing is a right of free speech.

Religious students must be permitted to display both political and religious slogans or logos on clothing, such as T-shirts or sweatshirts, when other students are permitted to wear clothing with similar messages or logos. When a school prohibits only religious slogans on students' clothing, the school is engaging in viewpoint discrimination and an unconstitutional interference with the students' right of free speech. A school may, on the other hand, prohibit all students from wearing message clothing. If that rule is applied equally to everyone, no matter whether the message is religious or secular, then religious students do not have the right to wear their religious clothing. Rules about clothing with messages must be uniform and must apply equally to everyone on a neutral basis. Religious or pro-life slogans may not be singled out for more hostile treatment.

Wearing message clothing is a right of free speech.

Students should be careful not to wear message clothing with language that denigrates other religions. This would be considered uncivil speech, which may be legally prohibited in school. In the same way, students may not use obscene speech or use their freedom of speech to promote illegal activity such as drug use.

School officials sometimes claim that certain speech—generally, proselytizing or pro-life messages—is offensive to others. However, a school may not curtail freedom of speech just because the message offends someone. Courts have held that if the message on clothing offends others, the viewers are free to avert their eyes and not look at the message. While some school officials have tried to ban pro-life speech as obscene, an objective definition of obscenity does not support this tactic.

May students organize Bible clubs at school?

If a public school takes federal financial assistance and allows one or more non-curricular related student groups to meet on school premises during non-instructional times, the federal Equal Access Act (EAA) makes it unlawful for the school to deny equal access to Christian students who wish to form a student Bible club. The right for Bible clubs to meet extends even into the elementary grades. Such clubs must be student-initiated and student-led. Schools that permit secular non-curricular clubs to meet must also permit students to conduct a non-curriculum related religious club on school premises during non-instructional time if the following conditions exist:

1. The meeting is voluntary and student-initiated;
2. There is no sponsorship of the meeting by the school, the government, or its agents or employees;
3. Employees or agents of the school or government are present at religious meetings only in a non-participatory capacity in order to maintain order;
4. The meeting does not materially and substantially interfere with the orderly conduct of educational activities within the school; and
5. Non-school persons do not direct, conduct, control, or regularly attend activities of student groups.

Students in great numbers have used the authority of the

Equal Access Act to form Bible clubs. Although the EAA was enacted in 1984 and declared to be constitutional by the United States Supreme Court in the Mergens case in1990, there are still some school officials who attempt to prohibit Bible clubs by claiming that all of the school's extracurricular activities are curriculum-related or that the school cannot provide supervision or space for the club. It is important to remember that unless a club is related to a subject matter area and the teacher requires attendance, gives assignments and grades, etc., the club is not curriculum-related. Virtually every public secondary school in the country has at least one non-curricular club operating on school grounds. Non-curricular groups include the football team.

> *The EAA requires that the Bible club be treated exactly like every other non-curricular club.*

Even when a Bible club is permitted, some school officials may attempt to limit the club's activities in illegal ways. Some schools seek to limit the club to meeting before or after school rather than during special club or lunch periods that are made available for other student clubs. Some schools seek to prohibit the Bible club from being pictured in the yearbook, from participating in club fairs, or from advertising its club meetings and activities. All of these prohibitions are illegal. The EAA requires that the Bible club be treated exactly like every other non-curricular club.

The following questions are commonly asked about Bible clubs. The answer to all of these questions is *yes*.

- May the club meet during lunch or scheduled club periods?
- May the club advertise its meetings on the same basis as other clubs even if Scripture verses are included in the advertisements?
- May the club have its picture in the yearbook?
- May club funds be included in school accounts that serve all non-curricular clubs equally?

There are only two ways for a school to escape the obligations of the Equal Access Act regarding Bible clubs. It may (1) cancel all non-curriculum related student groups (including the football team), or (2) forego all federal funding. When Bible clubs have a right to meet, they must be permitted to do everything other non-curricular clubs do. If other groups have access to the school newspaper, the yearbook, bulletin boards, the public address system, and the annual club fair, the Christian group must be given the same access.

In order for the religious activity to be protected by the Equal Access Act, the Bible club meeting must occur during non-instructional time, such as before or after school or during school lunch or club periods. The club must be initiated and run by the students, not by outsiders such as an area youth pastor. A club may occasionally invite an outside speaker, such as a local youth group pastor, to speak to the club. However, it is recommended that outside speakers be invited only about once a month and they should not always be the same person. If outside individuals, such as local youth pastors, want to assist the club, they should do so by meeting with club leaders after school at some non-school location such as a church or restaurant. The youth pastor can then assist the club leaders and train them to minister to their peers during the club meetings. Many youth pastors have found that such training actually strengthens the ministry gifts and spiritual maturity of the Bible club leaders.

Courts have also recognized that it is permissible for Bible clubs to have a requirement that all officers be Christians. The school administration may not prohibit religious qualifications for officers of the Bible club. Courts have wisely realized that prohibiting such requirements would negate the very purpose of the club.

It is permisssible for Bible clubs to have a requirement that all officers be Christians.

It is also worthy of note that Bible clubs are distinct from non-curricular or school-sponsored clubs in that an employee or other agent of the school may only be present at religious club meetings in a non-participatory capacity. This restriction does not apply to other school clubs, but is imposed on Bible clubs to avoid the appearance of an establishment of religion by the government. If the school needs to employ outside help in order to supervise the club and asks a parent, substitute teacher, or local pastor to serve as club advisor, that person then becomes an agent of the school and may not participate in the club's religious activities any more than a teacher could. The school's representative or club advisor is merely there to keep order and to serve as a contact person for the school.

May students use notebooks, pencils, and other material with religious logos or sayings, including Bible verses?

Students are permitted to use pencils, notebooks, book covers, etc. with religious logos or messages to the same extent that students may use such items with secular messages or logos. Students have free speech rights in school, and since free speech includes religious speech and includes the written as well as the spoken word, a student's right to use school supplies with religious messages is protected by the First Amendment Free Speech Clause.

In fact, one of the few remaining legal ways to bring the Ten Commandments into the classroom is to have the students do so either by posting them on their lockers (if students are permitted to place secular posters on their lockers) or by using book covers or other school supplies with the Ten Commandments printed on them. Many religious groups have made such supplies available to students through the Internet or though other means of distribution. While a school is not permitted to officially display the Ten Commandments for religious purposes, students have additional free speech rights in public schools that teachers, principals, or other staff do not have. Courts have held that a public school teacher must have some secular, curriculum-related purpose to be able to post the Ten Commandments alone in a public school. However, students are not restricted by the same legal prohibitions and may freely bring the Ten Commandments into the classroom on book covers or notebooks. Other religious messages are also permitted on school supplies, subject only to the prohibitions against uncivil or obscene speech that apply to all message clothing or equipment.

May students engage in group religious activities such as "See You at the Pole?"

Students are permitted to participate in non-official prayer events such as See You at the Pole (SYATP). SYATP is a student-initiated, student-led gathering of youth at their school flagpole, usually before the school day begins, to pray for their school, friends, teachers, government, and nation. Just like Bible clubs, these student-initiated and student-led prayer events are constitutionally protected free speech.

School officials may neither discourage nor encourage student participation in these events, nor may they prohibit the activities. The federal government has recognized the students' right to pray at SYATP gatherings and courts have regularly upheld this right when school officials have challenged it. Because it is constitutionally protected speech, the Supreme Court has held that student expressive activity—including prayer—may not be prohibited by the public school unless the activity creates an actual material and substantial disruption to the school's ability to fulfill its educational goals. If properly carried out, student prayer events would not cause such a disruption.

School authorities sometimes believe that allowing students to engage in any religious speech at school would be a violation of the Establishment Clause and its modern interpretation, which is sometimes called "the separation of church and state." This argument has been reviewed and rejected by the United States Supreme Court. Restricting or banning a SYATP event because it involves religious speech and prayer would violate the free speech rights of students and the constitutional requirement for neutral treatment of all student speech.

May a student mention religion in a graduation speech?

Even if student prayer is banned at graduation, students selected under a neutral criterion to deliver graduation messages, such as valedictorians and salutatorians, have free speech rights, including religious speech, under the federal Constitution. As long as the school chooses the graduation speaker using neutral selection criteria, such as grade point average or class officers, and as long as school officials have no official input into the student speech, the student speaker has a right to discuss anything that is not uncivil, illegal, proselytizing or obscene. This area of law, however, is still unsettled, and some courts have upheld the right of schools to ban religious speech, even by students, at graduation.

Courts recognize a clear constitutional difference between officially controlled speech about religion in public schools and spontaneous student religious speech.

Certainly, the student graduation speaker should keep in mind both the audience and the occasion for the speech. However, where school officials do not control the speech, courts have generally held that it is constitutionally permissible for the student to mention religion. Courts recognize a clear constitutional difference between officially controlled speech about religion in public schools and spontaneous or private student religious speech. Official speech about religion is unconstitutional under the modern Establishment Clause doctrine of "separation of church and state." Student religious speech, whether in an address prepared by the student ahead of time, or in a spontaneous and extemporaneous remark added to the end of a pre-approved graduation speech, is protected under the Free Speech Clause of the First Amendment. Graduation ceremonies are discussed at greater length in the Curriculum section of this resource.

Must students be permitted to wear modest dress in gym class if their religion requires it?

Because there is no compelling reason for a local school district to force all students to wear one particular style of gym clothes; or to take one particular gym class, such as swimming, students must be permitted to adapt their dress to their religious beliefs. This need for religious accommodation generally arises when a female student is forced to wear shorts or slacks for gym class or to participate in a mixed swimming class. The school is required to accommodate a student's religious beliefs and permit her to wear gym clothes that will satisfy her religious beliefs while still permitting her to participate in some sort of physical activity. Often the compromise attire is culottes, bicycle shorts or sweat pants worn under a skirt. In the case of a religious objection to mixed swimming, the school must provide an alternative gym class or activity for either boys or girls.

The school is permitted to require the student to change clothes for gym class as long as the clothing is acceptable to the student's religious requirements. Courts have held that imposing a requirement for immodest dress or activity upon religious students violates their First Amendment right to the free exercise of religion. Courts have also required schools to accommodate a religious student's conviction against any coeducational physical education classes because the school is always able to provide individual physical education for the student.

May students be permitted to use religious material in a school talent show?

For the same reason that students are permitted to choose religious topics for class assignments, they are also permitted to choose religious material for a school talent show. Students are consumers of government education; they are not agents of the state, as are teachers and school officials. Only a teacher's or other school official's actions with regard to religion could violate the Establishment Clause.

A student's actions, such as choosing a religious presentation for a school talent show, can never violate the Establishment Clause. However, prohibiting a child from making such a choice would violate the child's right to free expression, including religious expression, under the First Amendment. By permitting a religious performance by a student, the school is demonstrating neutrality, not an endorsement of religion.

Censorship of a child's choice of talent for anything other than obscenity, illegality, or profanity violates basic non-discrimination and neutrality principles. As the *Presidential Guidelines on Student Expression in Public Schools* indicate, God has not been totally banned from public schools; teachers have merely been banned from proselytizing as government agents.

May students talk about religion in class discussions?

Students may ask questions or even challenge a teacher's viewpoint in class if the student's question or comment is directly related to the ongoing classroom discussion and is not disruptive. While a student could not stand up in a science class and give a salvation sermon, that student could clearly ask a question challenging the scientific basis for evolution or presenting a scientific argument for an alternate scientific position. As long as a religious comment is pertinent to the topic being discussed in the classroom, a religious student may give a religious opinion in the same manner as other students may give secular opinions during an open classroom discussion.

A student is also free to decline to answer a question on a test that would require him to violate his sincerely held religious beliefs. For instance, the teacher might pose a test question asking students to give reasons why the Bible is not true or why evolution is true. Religious students may respond to such questions in several ways. They could answer the question in the manner the teacher is anticipating and then write an explanatory note distancing themselves from that viewpoint. They could also write a note explaining why they do not agree with the answer the teacher expects, but also providing the teacher's required answer.

The teacher may not lower a student's grade because of his religious objection to answering a test question in a manner that would violate his religious beliefs. In fact, good teachers should be sufficiently aware of the religious beliefs of all students in the classroom that they would not ask a question that would place any student in such an untenable position.

Key Cases Supporting Student Free Speech and Free Exercise Rights in Public Schools

Landmark Cases Supporting Student Free Speech in Public School

West Virginia Bd. of Educ. v. Barnette, 319 U.S. 624, (1943).

The Supreme Court held that the state could not force public school students, in this case Jehovah's Witnesses, to say the pledge of allegiance in class because a religious adherent may not be compelled to participate in a flag salute in violation of his rights of conscience. The Court was intending to protect Jehovah's Witnesses and other religious minorities from official coercion; however, the Court did not prohibit the flag salute for all students merely because a minority of children opposed it. The school was merely required to recognize an individual student's right to refrain from speaking and the fact that the government may not compel a person to speak about, endorse, or subsidize topics that are objectionable to that person. The Court said:

> That [schools] are educating the young for citizenship is reason for scrupulous protection of Constitutional freedoms of the individual, if we are not to strangle the free mind at its source and teach youth to discount important principles of our government as mere platitudes.

The Supreme Court also emphasized:

> If there is any fixed star in our constitutional constellation, it is that no official, high or petty, can prescribe what shall be orthodox in politics, nationalism, religion, or other matters of opinion or force citizens to confess by word or act their faith therein.

Tinker v. Des Moines Indep. Community Sch. Dist., 393 U.S. 503 (1969).

This is the key case supporting the free speech rights of students in public schools. The Supreme Court plainly declared that public school students do not leave their rights of free speech at the schoolhouse gate; students do not forfeit their First Amendment rights to free speech simply by attending public school.

The Court said: "It can hardly be argued that either students or teachers shed their constitutional rights to freedom of speech or expression at the schoolhouse gate." This protection extends "from Kindergarten through high school." The Court said that a student's free speech rights apply "when [they are] in the cafeteria, or on the playing field, or on the campus during the authorized hours. "

Because student expressive activity is protected by the First Amendment, student speech cannot be prohibited by a public school unless the activity creates a material and substantial disruption to the school's ability to fulfill its academic purpose. Such speech may not be restricted where there has been "no finding and no showing that engaging [in the activity] would materially and substantially interfere with the requirements of appropriate discipline in the operation of the school."

This standard of "material and substantial disruption" cannot be met merely by the *possibility* of disruption. The Court held that "in our system, undifferentiated fear or apprehension of disturbance is not enough to overcome the right to freedom of expression."

The Court recognized the unique constitutional position of students who are required to attend school:

> [I]n our system, state operated schools may not be enclaves for totalitarianism. School officials do not possess absolute authority over their students. Students in school as well as out of school are persons under our Constitution. They are possessed of fundamental rights which the state must respect, just as they themselves must respect their obligations to the state. In our system, students may not be regarded as closed circuit recipients of only that which the state chooses to communicate. They may not be confined to the expressions of those sentiments that are officially approved.

This fundamental constitutional principle is applicable both inside and outside the classroom. The *Tinker* Court made clear that when a student "is in the cafeteria, or on the playing field, or on the campus during the authorized hours, he may express his opinions."

Board of Educ. v. Mergens, 496 U.S. 226 (1990).

In this second landmark United States Supreme Court case discussing student rights of free speech and free exercise in public schools, the Court upheld the Equal Access Act that Congress had passed in order to permit students to hold Bible Clubs for religious expression in public schools.

The Court made very clear that protecting the free religious speech and free exercise rights of students in a public school would not present any Establishment Clause problem:

> Petitioners' principal contention is that the [Equal Access] Act has the primary effect of advancing religion. Specifically, petitioners urge that, because the student religious meetings are held under school aegis, and because the state's compulsory attendance laws bring the students together (and thereby provide a ready-made audience for student evangelists), an objective observer in the position of a secondary school student will perceive official school support for such religious meetings. . . . We disagree.

The reason student religious speech does not violate the Establishment Clause is because it is private speech, not official school speech, and private speech can never violate the Establishment Clause:

> As Justice O'Connor stated: "There is a crucial difference between *government* speech endorsing religion, which the Establishment Clause forbids, and *private* speech endorsing religion, which the Free Speech and Free Exercise Clauses protect."

The Supreme Court stated that a state institution, such as a public school, must protect student religious speech, and that religion has not been banned from public schools. The key to the correct application of the law is neutrality. The Court said:

> The message is one of neutrality rather than endorsement . . . . The Establishment Clause does not license government to treat religion and those who teach or practice it, simply by virtue of their status as such, as subversive of American ideals and therefore subject to unique disabilities.

Finally, the Court held that the Equal Access Act, 20 U.S.C. § 4071 (1984), mandates that schools receiving federal funds must give student religious clubs equal access to advertising outlets, yearbooks, and school fairs—as well as any other venues in which non-religious clubs participate.

Morse v. Frederick, 552 U.S. 393 (2007).

In a 5-4 decision, the Supreme Court ruled that public schools have the right to discipline students for certain types of speech (previously limited to obscene speech). This case involved an Alaska high school principal who suspended a student for displaying a banner with the message "BONG HITS 4 JESUS" during a school activity. The principal reasonably thought the sign was intended to promote drug use, which violated the school's mission. Chief Justice Roberts, writing for the Court's majority, said: "We hold that schools may take steps to safeguard those entrusted to their care from speech that can be reasonably regarded as encouraging illegal drug use." Justice Thomas has a brilliant concurring opinion in this case, portions of which are included later in this book.

Other Cases Supporting Student Religious Expression in Public Schools

Grayned v. City of Rockford, 408 U.S. 104 (1972).

School property or adjacent public sidewalks "may not be declared off limits for expressive activity for students," unless it materially disrupts classwork or invades the rights of others (citing *Tinker*).

Chandler v. McMinnville Sch. Dist., 978 F.2d 524 (9th Cir. 1982).

The court held that official school-sponsored speech is reviewed under the *Hazelwood* (see below) standard, while student speech is reviewed under the *Tinker* standard. Buttons students wore on their clothing were held to be student speech, and could not be confused with school-sponsored speech.

Clark v. Dallas Ind. Sch. Dist., 806 F. Supp. 116 (N.D. Tex. 1992).

A school may not prohibit student speech merely because another student objects to the content of the message. The court held: "If school officials were permitted to prohibit expression to which other students objected, absent any further justification, the officials would have a license to prohibit virtually every type of expression." Mere disagreement with the content of speech is not a sufficient reason to deny student speech.

Rosenberger v. Rector and Visitors of the Univ. of Virginia, 515 U.S. 819 (1995).

The state must treat religious groups and non-religious groups the same in use of funds for publishing newspapers. To deny this fundamental principle would be to eviscerate the essential guarantees of free speech and religious freedom under the First Amendment.

Mitchell v. Helms, 350 U.S. 793 (2000).

The Supreme Court requires equal treatment of and neutrality towards religion in schools; and such equal treatment does not violate the Establishment Clause.

Key Cases Prohibiting Official School-Sponsored Religious Speech

Hazelwood School District v. Kuhlmeier, 484 U.S. 260 (1988).

An official school publication that is part of the curriculum, such as a school newspaper, is not student speech, but official school speech. Therefore, its content may be controlled by the school. The Court also held that a school may prohibit speech that is sexually explicit, libelous, or defamatory toward another student.

Santa Fe Independent School District v. Doe, 530 U.S. 290 (2000).

The Supreme Court declared that official school prayers are unconstitutional at football games. An official Texas school district policy both encouraged and permitted students to offer prayers before home football games. The school district controlled the amplification during the giving of the prayers, including the ability to cut off the microphone. A lawsuit filed against the school district in federal court claimed the district's policies and practices violated the Establishment Clause of the First Amendment. The United States Supreme Court agreed and decided that such officially-sponsored prayers were unconstitutional under the Establishment Clause (now often referred to as the modern legal doctrine of the "separation of church and state"). Even though the students offered the prayers, the Court said that the prayers were government sponsored because of the official school policy and the planned use of the school's amplification equipment. These factors, said the Court, constituted official speech by the school, not free speech by the student. Therefore, these "official" prayers before games were not protected student speech.

The Court did make clear, however, that "nothing in the Constitution as interpreted by this Court prohibits any public school student from voluntarily praying at any time before, during, or after the school day."

Bannon v. School Dist. of Palm Beach County, 387 F.3d 1208 (11th Cir. 2004).

The school allowed students to paint panels of a mural in the school for a small fee. Some students chose to paint murals with religious symbols and expressions, which generated some media attention and controversy in the school. School officials asked the students to paint over the offending (religious) portions of the mural. The court ruled that because the murals were school-sponsored, the school could censor them based on viewpoint for legitimate pedagogical purposes. Note that in similar cases, other courts have determined that in situations where students or families purchase bricks or tiles for fund raising or other purposes, the school has created a limited public forum and free expression, including individual religious expression, must be permitted.

Cases Impacting Student Religious Speech in Public School

Widmar v. Vincent, 454 U.S. 263 (1981).

A public university that allowed student groups to use its facilities for meetings created a limited open forum, and could not deny any group meeting space based on viewpoint, which would violate the free speech rights of students. The right of student free speech includes religious speech, so the university could not forbid a religious student group to use its facilities on the same basis as others.

Bethel School District v. Fraser, 478 U.S. 675 (1986).

Public schools may control the content of student speeches or student newspapers for legitimate pedagogical purposes or for obscenity. In this case, the student delivered an obscene nominating speech during a student assembly, and his speech was not protected.

Poling v. Murphy, 872 F.2d 757 (6th Cir. 1989).

The school is permitted to ban speech that is obscene speech or speech that is violent or crude or lacks "civility." This case was also about an offensive speech delivered by a student running for a school office. The court held that the school could discipline the student under such circumstances. This case did not answer the question of just what would constitute a lack of civility in speech.

Capitol Square Review and Advisory Bd. v. Pinette, 515 U.S. 753 (1995).

The Supreme Court stated:

> Our precedent establishes that private religious speech, far from being a First Amendment orphan, is as fully protected under the Free Speech Clause as secular private expression . . . Indeed, in Anglo-American history, at least, government-

suppression of speech has so commonly been directed precisely at religious speech that a free-speech clause without religion would be Hamlet without the prince.

Fleming v. Jefferson County School Dist. R-1, 298 F.3d 918 (10th Cir. 2002).

When the school invited a select group of people to paint tiles to be part of an artistic display in the school after a high school shooting, the school did not open up a public forum and could therefore impose guidelines on the tiles' content. For example, the school could decline to post tiles that contained the date of the shooting, names of students, gang symbols, or religious words and symbols (reading Hazelwood to mean schools may discriminate based on viewpoint when speech is school-sponsored). Note again that where courts determine that schools have created a limited open forum with such projects, religious speech may not be prohibited.

Hansen v. Ann Arbor Public Schools, 293 F. Supp. 2d 780 (E.D. Mich. 2003).

When the student-lead Gay/Straight Alliance club organized a discussion panel for "Diversity Week" comprised only of pro-homosexual clergy leaders, a Christian student asked to either participate or to have her viewpoint that homosexual behavior is sin represented by a cleric she nominated. The school denied her request, and censored her "Diversity Week" speech in which she wanted to express the view that religion and sexual orientation differ from race because they are not inborn characteristics. The court ruled that the "Diversity Week" presentations were school-sponsored speech; therefore, the school could not suppress one viewpoint of an issue while allowing the promotion of another (rejecting Fleming's reading of Hazelwood).

Phillips v. Oxford Separate Mun. School Dist., 314 F. Supp. 2d 643 (N.D.Miss. 2003).

A candidate for student government office used a religious

symbol and reference on a campaign poster that otherwise met all the size and location requirements imposed by the school. The poster raised controversy among the teachers and students, and the school removed the poster in response to complaints. The court ruled that the school probably did not violate the student's free expression rights by removing the poster because the school had "legitimate pedagogical interests" in removing a source of controversy and the student had other methods of campaigning available. This court did not take into consideration the legal concept of a "heckler's veto" which prohibits opponents from interfering with another's free speech rights. Nor did it consider the fact that generally in free speech law offense may not limit free speech rights. Finally, this court did not recognize a traditional free speech legal concept that the response to speech with which we disagree is not censorship, but more speech.

Cases Involving Student Distribution of Religious Material in School

Martin v. Struthers, 319 U.S. 141 (1943).

The right to freedom of speech has always included the right to distribute written tracts, including religious tracts.

Thomas v. Collins, 323 U.S. 516 (1945).

The Court held that the "free trade of ideas means . . . the opportunity to persuade, not merely to describe facts."

Riseman v. School Committee, 439 F.2d 148 (1st Cir. 1971).

The court invalidated a school policy requiring students to have literature approved before distribution.

Eisner v. Stamford Bd. of Educ., 440 F.2d 803 (2nd Cir. 1971).

A prior review policy was considered by the court to be a prior restraint on speech that could only be permitted if accompanied by elaborate procedural safeguards to insure the free flow of speech.

Quarterman v. Byrd, 453 F.2d 54 (4th Cir. 1971).

A rule was unconstitutional which required any prior permission from the principal before distributing any literature.

Fujishima v. Board of Educ., 460 F.2d 1355 (7th Cir. 1972).

A school's policy requiring review of literature before distribution by a student violated the First Amendment. The court held: "In no way may students be required to announce their intentions of engaging in certain conduct beforehand so school authorities may decide whether to prohibit the conduct."

Erznoznik v. City of Jacksonville, 422 U.S. 205 (1975).

Courts have consistently held, using general free speech

principles, that offense is never a reason to limit free speech.

United States v. Grace, 461 U.S. 171 (1983).

The Court held that leafletting is protected speech under the First Amendment.

Thompson v. Waynesboro Area Sch. Dist., 673 F. Supp. 1379, (M.D. Pa. 1987).

If a school restricts student literature distribution to areas outside the school building, that restriction violates students' free speech rights.

Burch v. Barker, 861 F.2d 1149 (9th Cir. 1988).

Schools must make a distinction between literature produced for pedagogical purposes and literature distributed by individual students. Schools in many states have specifically allowed distribution of the Christian newsletter, *Issues and Answers*, in all public schools.

Rivera v. Board of Regents, 721 F. Supp. 1189 (D. Colo. 1989).

A policy permitting prior review of literature to be distributed by students was unconstitutional because school officials retained "unfettered discretion." The policy "gave school officials the power to extinguish the rights of students to speak through inaction and delay." This court also rejected the school's Establishment Clause defense stating:

> The Establishment Clause is a limitation on the power of governments; it is not a restriction on the rights of individuals acting in their private lives. . . . There is a distinction between school-affiliated speech and the private speech of students. It is clear that the mere fact that student speech occurs on school property does not make it government supported.

Slotterback v. Interboro Sch. Dist., 766 F. Supp. 280 (E.D. Pa. 1991).

Student distribution of literature in a public school is protected by the First Amendment. The court held, quoting *Tinker*:

> Public schools are, in part, to accommodate students during prescribed hours for personal intercommunication. Unless the students' speech is curriculum-related, the speech cannot be limited during those hours on the school campus without a strong showing of interference with school activities or with the rights of other students. As the [U.S. Supreme] Court stated, "Dedication to specific uses [including student interpersonal communication] does not imply that the constitutional rights of persons entitled to be there are to be gauged as if the premises were purely private property.

ISKCON. v. Lee, 505 U.S. 672 (1992).

The Supreme Court has long recognized that "the right to distribute flyers and literature lies at the heart of the liberties guaranteed by the Speech and Press Clauses of the First Amendment to the United States Constitution."

Hedges v. Wauconda Comm. Unit Sch. Dist. No. 118, 9 F.3d 1295 (7th Cir. 1993).

The court permitted a school to restrict the distribution of more than ten copies of written material prepared by non-students to a table in the hallway because this time, place, and manner restriction neutrally applied to all material, whether religious or non-religious.

Johnston-Loehner v. O'Brien, 859 F. Supp. 575 (M.D. Fla. 1994).

A school may not preview literature for content before permitting distribution. The court said:

> In order for the State in the person of school officials to justify prohibition of a particular expression of opinion, it must be able to show that its action was caused by something more than a mere desire to avoid the discomfort and unpleasantness that always accompany an unpopular viewpoint.

The school must show that the distribution would materially and substantially interfere with school operations or with the rights of other students. The school could not require that literature only be placed in a predetermined location.

Muller v. Jefferson Lighthouse Sch., 98 F.3d 1530 (7th Cir. 1996), cert. denied, 520 U.S. 1156 (1997).

The court held that an elementary school principal could review invitations to a religious meeting for offensive content prior to their distribution by a student. On the other hand, courts have permitted teachers to distribute invitations to religious meetings in class along with other notices of outside activities for students, as long as the notices contain only the time, place, date, and sponsor of the meeting and do not contain Bible verses or proselytizing material.

Walz ex rel. Walz v. Egg Harbor Tp. Bd. of Educ., 342 F.3d 271 (3rd Cir. 2003).

A school policy prohibiting the distribution of proselytizing pencils and evangelical candy canes during school parties did not violate the students' First Amendment rights to freedom of speech, especially when the students are young elementary age and may not be able to discern private free speech from official school viewpoints. Courts will take into account the context and students' age when evaluating the reasonableness of such school policies. However, see the case below, which reached an opposite conclusion.

Westfield High School L.I.F.E. Club v. City of Westfield, 249 F. Supp. 2d 98 (D. Mass 2003).

Members of a Christian club at a public school defied a principal's refusal to allow them to distribute candy canes with a Gospel message attached and were suspended. The court ruled that a school may have a policy requiring prior approval of anything students wish to distribute as private speech, but that policy must be narrowly drawn, have a quick review process, and may only reject content on the basis of its likelihood of causing a disruption to education. This school's policy did not meet those requirements and was thus invalid.

Walker-Serrano v. Lackawanna Trail Elementary School, 325 F.3d 412 (3rd Cir. 2003).

Amanda Walker-Serrano was a third-grader who objected to a school trip to the circus because of the mistreatment of circus animals. School officials decided they had a right to prevent this elementary school student from circulating a petition to her fellow students on behalf of the animals. All three federal judges agreed that even elementary students have some rights to freedom of expression, while they disagreed on the extent of those rights. But all three judges agreed that Amanda did have the right to distribute free literature to her peers at school even if she did not have the right in an elementary school to collect names on a petition. The only question on which the court was divided was whether an elementary student could collect signatures on a petition in an elementary school.

Several other factors in this case are relevant to literature distribution by students in public schools:

1. Amanda was circulating her petition in the classroom as well as on the playground (where one child may have been injured while signing it). A school has more control over free speech expression in the classroom than it does in the hallways, on the playground or in the lunchroom.

2. The matter at issue in this case was the circulation of a petition. Amanda's free speech right to distribute free literature to her classmates (she later distributed coloring books and stickers regarding animal rights) was never in question.

Curry ex rel. Curry v. Sch. Dist., 452 F. Supp. 2d 723 (E.D. Mich. 2006).

The court ruled that it was First Amendment protected free speech when a student provided explanations about the religious significance of candy canes to other students.

M.B. ex rel. Martin v. Liverpool Cent. Sch. Dist., 487 F. Supp. 2d 117 (N.D.N.Y. 2007).

The court ruled that the school district violated the First Amendment free speech rights of an elementary school student when it refused to allow her to distribute a flyer about her relationship with Jesus Christ to her friends during non-instructional time since her speech was private student speech and could not be attributed to the school district. The school had banned distribution of the flyers because they were religious, but officials could not demonstrate that the distribution materially or substantially interfered with the school's operation or with the rights of other students.

Raker v. Frederick County Public Schools, 470 F. Supp. 2d 634 (W.D. Va. 2007).

The distribution of pro-life literature by students during non-instructional times was First Amendment protected speech.

Lowery v. Euverard, 397 F.3d 584 (6th Cir. 2007).

The court permitted a school to remove players from the football team after they circulated a petition saying that they hated the coach and would not play for him.

M.A.L. ex rel. M.L. v. Kinsland, 543 F.3d 841 (6th Cir. 2008).

The court reversed a district court opinion and upheld a school district's neutral time, place and manner regulation against distribution of material in school hallways. Therefore, the school district legitimately barred a student's distribution of pro-life material in the hallway. The school could require pre-approval of the material because the school's policy was content neutral and was not based on viewpoint. The school would have permitted the student to post the pro-life material on a hallway bulletin board or distribute it from a table in the cafeteria.

Florey v. Sioux Falls School Dist., 619 F.2d 1311 (8th Cir. 1980), cert denied, 499 U.S. 987 (1980).

The Sioux Falls school district policy upheld by the court was a policy that protected students' religious expression of belief or non-belief in "composition, art forms, music, speech and debate." This policy is included in the Curriculum section of this book.

DeNooyer v. Livonia Pub. Sch., 799 F. Supp. 744 (E.D. Mich. 1992), aff'd, 12 F.3d 211 (6th Cir. 1993), *cert. denied*, 511 U.S. 1031 (1994).

A teacher did not violate a second grader's First Amendment right to free expression when she prohibited the student from showing a videotape of herself singing a religious song in church to her second grade classmates during "show and tell." The teacher's primary pedagogical concern was to increase her students' verbal communication skills by requiring a "live" classroom presentation by the student on some subject of the student's choosing. That concern was frustrated by the student showing a videotape of a previous presentation at another location. The pedagogical concern, not the religious nature of the videotape, was a unique factor in the assignment and in the court's decision.

Settle v. Dickson County Sch. Bd., 53 F.3d 152 (6th Cir. 1995).

The court upheld a teacher's right to give a student a zero for a research paper on Jesus Christ because the teacher said the paper did not fit the research topic assigned. Students had been instructed to research a topic they did not previously know anything about.

Baldwinsville School District, TX v. Peck, 426 F.3d 617 (5th Cir. 2005).

The U.S. Supreme Court let stand this lower court decision permitting public schools to display religious posters made by students. The school may not censor the religious viewpoints of students who use religious themes in school assignments. The teacher had told her kindergarten class to draw a poster about the environment. When Anthony Peck included a picture of Jesus praying for the environment in his drawing, school officials refused to display the boy's artwork without folding back the section that pictured Jesus, claiming that portion of the picture violated the separation of church and state. The court did not agree, holding that students are permitted to use religious themes when their teachers give them a choice of assignment topics and the picture could be displayed without violating the Establishment Clause.

O.T. ex rel. Turton v. Frenchtown Elementary Sch. Dist., 465 F. Supp. 2d 369 (D.N.J. 2006).

The court held that the school district had engaged in impermissible viewpoint discrimination in violation of First Amendment free speech rights when it refused to allow an elementary school student to sing "Awesome God" at a school talent show.

Busch v. Marple Newtown Sch. Dist., 567 F.3d 89 (2009).

A Kindergarten teacher featured a different student each week in a unit called "All About Me" and permitted students to make posters about their families, hobbies and interests. Parents were invited to participate. Wesley Busch's mother wanted to read from the Bible, Wesley's favorite book. The court ruled that Wesley's free speech rights were not violated when his mother's Bible presentation was disallowed. Wesley was permitted to include a picture of his church on his poster.

Cases Impacting Religious Accommodation and Opt Out Rights

West Virginia State Bd. of Educ. v. Barnette, 319 U.S. 624 (1943).

In considering a Jehovah's Witness child whose sincerely held religious belief conflicted with the requirement that students salute the flag, the United States Supreme Court ruled that public schools must excuse students from participating in activities that would violate their religious beliefs (as expressed by their parents). The Court did not require that the activity be discontinued for everyone.

Moody v. Cronin, 484 F. Supp. 270 (C.D. Ill. 1979).

In this case the issue as stated by the court was whether the state denied students their freedom of religion by "compelling children of the United Pentecostal Church who attend public schools in Illinois to attend all coeducational physical education classes under penalty of suspension, expulsion, denial of credits for graduation and other discipline." The court found that the students had a sincere religious belief against co-ed gym classes, including the immodest dress imposed upon the students and the occasional physical contact between the sexes in their P.E. activities. The court held:

> The compulsory attendance at a coeducational physical education class is in sharp conflict with the fundamental mode of life mandated by the Pentecostal religion. It is obvious that compulsory attendance has engendered great concern and conflict in the family. Under the present facts there is, through coeducational physical education, daily exposure of the children to worldly influences in terms of attitudes and values of dress contrary to their religious beliefs. This exposure also substantially interferes with the religious development of the Pentecostal children and their integration into the way of life of the Pentecostal faith community at the crucial adolescent stage of development.

Mozert v. Hawkins County Bd. of Educ., 827 F.2d 1058 (6th Cir. 1987).

Several Christian middle and elementary school students and/or their parents objected to a new reading text series the school adopted because they believed the series contained anti-Christian-themed stories and values. The court ruled that the reading materials did not coerce the students or parents to violate their religion, and that citizens' wishes could not dictate government officials' actions with regard to curriculum; however, parents could request an opt out for their individual students.

Morrison ex rel. Morrison v. Board of Educ. of Boyd County, Kentucky, 507 F.3 494 (6th. Cir. 2008).

A school provided mandatory "diversity tolerance training" regarding homosexuality. The court ruled that requiring attendance for the anti-harassment class would not have violated the students' religious beliefs, and no student free speech rights were violated for prohibiting anti-harassing language against homosexual students.

Broussard v. Sch. Brd. of City of Norfolk, 801 F. Supp. 1526 (E.D. Va. 1992).

Student speech, including message shirts, may be banned if the expression is lewd or obscene.

McIntire v. Betel Sch., 804 F. Supp. 1415 (W.D. Okla. 1992).

Message shirts may be banned if the clothing has slogans specifically advertising alcoholic beverages.

Chalifoux v. New Caney Indep. Sch. Dist., 976 F. Supp. 659 (S.D. Tex. 1997).

The court held that students could wear rosary necklaces to school because wearing such necklaces was a form of religious free expression protected by the First Amendment.

Nixon v. Northern Local School Dist. Bd. of Educ., 383 F.Supp.2d 965 (S.D. Ohio 2005).

Religious statements about homosexuality, Islam, and abortion on a tee shirt were not inherently "explicit, vulgar, and plainly offensive words," and a T-shirt message stating "homosexuality is sin" could not be banned unless the school could demonstrate that the ban was motivated by a fear that the message would actually disrupt the educational process. The fear of disruption cannot be mere speculation that other students might be offended, but must be demonstrable history of disrupting conflict over the topics in question.

Harper v. Poway Unified School Dist., 445 F.3d 1166 (9th Cir. 2006).

After the gay-rights Day of Silence, a student wore a tee shirt with a hand-written slogan expressing God's disapproval of homosexuality. The school had a history of disruptions and altercations regarding sexual orientation, so the court ruled that the school could forbid the student from wearing the shirt in the interest of avoiding disruption of the educational process. Where actual disruption could not be shown (or where only one side was causing the disruption), the outcome would presumably be different.

Jacobs v. Clark County School Dist., 526 F.3d 419 (9th Cir. 2008).

A high school student claimed the school dress code requiring uniforms did not allow the free expression of religious views on a message T-shirt. The court ruled that a school dress code requiring school uniforms is viewpoint neutral and, therefore, did not violate the free expression of religious speech by disallowing all message T-shirts.

Key Cases Regarding Equal Access Clubs

Board of Educ. v. Mergens, 496 U.S. 226 (1990).

In response to numerous complaints that public schools were discriminating against student religious clubs, the United States Congress passed the Equal Access Act ("EAA") in 1984. The Act is included later in this section.

If a public school receives federal funds and allows one or more non-curriculum-related student groups to meet on the school campus (which would include a football team), the school may not prohibit or deny equal access to other non-curriculum-related student groups, including student Bible clubs.

The *Mergens* Court ruled that a public school also violated the EAA when it denied a Christian club equal access to accommodations made available to other non-curriculum student clubs, such as the school newspaper, bulletin boards, public address system, and annual club fair. Other non-curriculum-related clubs that were officially recognized by the school included a scuba diving club, chess club, and a special education service club.

The Court interpreted a "non-curriculum-related student group" to mean "any student group that does not directly relate to the body of courses offered by the school." It held:

> [A] student group directly relates to a school's curriculum if the subject matter of the group is actually taught, or will soon be taught, in a regularly offered course; if the subject matter of the group concerns the body of courses as a whole; if the participation in the group is required for a particular course; or if participation in the group results in academic credit.

The EAA requires a public school to make meeting space equally available to non-curriculum-related groups on school grounds at equally reasonable times.

Pope v. East Brunswick Bd. of Educ., 12 F.3d 1244 (3rd Cir. 1993).

Denying a Bible club equal access to meeting facilities and

other benefits enjoyed by other clubs violated the EAA because other non-curriculum-related clubs were allowed to meet on school premises.

Garnett v. Renton School District, 987 F.2d 641 (9th Cir. 1993).

The Equal Access Act preempts any conflicting state laws, thus school officials could not prevent the formation of a student-led Bible club under a conflicting state law.

Sease v. School District of Philadelphia, 811 F. Supp. 183 (E.D. Pa. 1993).

The Equal Access Act prohibited a school employee's active participation in a student religious group. Therefore, the court did not consider the employee's First Amendment claims.

Hsu v. Roslyn Union Free School Dist. No. 3, 85 F.3d 839 (2d Cir. 1996), *cert. denied*, Roslyn Union Free Sch. Dist. No. 3 v. Hsu, 519 U.S. 1040 (1996).

Under the Equal Access Act, a school district may not interfere with a leadership policy provision in the Constitution of a religious club that excludes non-Christians from leadership positions that involve leading Christian prayers and devotions and safeguarding the "spiritual content" of the meetings. The court agreed that requiring the non-discrimination policy would essentially obliterate the unique essence of the Christian club. Having Christian leaders necessarily shapes the content of the religious speech at the meetings because the nature and quality of the speech at the meetings is dependent upon the religious commitment of the officers.

Herdahl v. Pontotoc County School District, 933 F. Supp. 582 (N.D. Miss. 1996).

The court permitted students in grades K-6 to meet for student-initiated prayer and Bible reading with a teacher present in the room but not participating.

Ceniceros v. Board of Trustees of the San Diego Unified School Dist., 106 F.3d 878 (9th Cir. 1997).

Denying a student religious club the opportunity to meet in classrooms during the high school lunch break, as other clubs were allowed to meet, violated the rights of the student religious club members under the Equal Access Act. A lunch hour during which no classroom instruction occurs is "non-instructional time" within the meaning of the Equal Access Act.

Prince v. Jacoby, 303 F.3d 1074 (9th Cir. 2002).

The EAA requires equal access for a Bible club to student funding, yearbook, public address system, bulletin boards, school supplies, and audio/visual equipment.

Donovan ex rel. Donovan v. Punxsutawney Area School Bd., 336 F.3d 211 (3rd Cir. 2004).

If other non-instructional student groups are allowed to meet during an "activity period," Bible clubs must be allowed to meet during that period, too, even if it is during school hours.

Cases Involving See You at the Pole (SYATP)

Hedges v. Wauconda Community Sch. Dist., 9 F.3d 1295 (7th Cir. 1993).

Restricting or banning SYATP because it involves religious prayer and worship would violate the constitutional requirement of neutrality.

Daugherty v. Vanguard Charter Academy, 116 F. Supp.2d 897 (W.D. Mich. 2000).

A federal district court rejected a legal challenge to SYATP, holding that voluntary student-initiated prayer at the school flagpole was entirely permissible.

Letter From Richard W. Riley, the Secretary United States Department of Education (May 1998)

Dear American Educator,

Almost three years ago, President Clinton directed me, as U.S. Secretary of Education, in consultation with the Attorney General, to provide every public school district in America with a statement of principles addressing the extent to which religious expression and activity are permitted in our public schools. In accordance with the President's directive, I sent every school superintendent in the country guidelines on Religious Expression in Public Schools in August of 1995.

The purpose of promulgating these presidential guidelines was to end much of the confusion regarding religious expression in our nation's public schools that had developed over more than thirty years since the U.S. Supreme Court decision in 1962 regarding state sponsored school prayer. I believe that these guidelines have helped school officials, teachers, students and parents find a new common ground on the important issue of religious freedom consistent with constitutional requirements.

In July of 1996, for example, the Saint Louis School Board adopted a district wide policy using these guidelines. While the school district had previously allowed certain religious activities, it had never spelled them out before, resulting in a lawsuit over the right of a student to pray before lunch in the cafeteria. The creation of a clearly defined policy using the guidelines allowed the school board and the family of the student to arrive at a mutually satisfactory settlement.

In a case decided last year in a United States District Court in Alabama, (Chandler v. James) involving student initiated prayer at school related events, the court instructed the DeKalb County School District to maintain for circulation in the library of each school a copy of the presidential guidelines.

The great advantage of the presidential guidelines, however, is that they allow school districts to avoid contentious disputes by developing a common understanding among students, teachers, parents and the broader community that the First Amendment does in fact provide ample room for religious expression by students while at the same time maintaining freedom from government sponsored religion.

The development and use of these presidential guidelines were not and are not isolated activities. Rather, these guidelines are part of an ongoing and growing effort by educators and America's religious community to find a new common ground. In April of 1995, for example, thirty-five religious groups issued "Religion in the Public Schools: A Joint Statement of Current Law" that the Department drew from in developing its own guidelines. Following the release of the presidential guidelines, the National PTA and the Freedom Forum jointly published in 1996 "A Parent's Guide to Religion in the Public Schools" which put the guidelines into an easily understandable question and answer format.

In the last two years, I have held three religious-education summits to inform faith communities and educators about the guidelines and to encourage continued dialogue and cooperation within constitutional limits. Many religious communities have contacted local schools and school systems to offer their assistance because of the clarity provided by the guidelines. The United Methodist Church has provided reading tutors to many schools, and Hadassah and the Women's League for Conservative Judaism have both been extremely active in providing local schools with support for summer reading programs.

The guidelines we are releasing today are the same as originally issued in 1995, except that changes have been made in the sections on religious excusals and student garb to reflect the Supreme Court decision in Boerne v. Flores declaring the Religious Freedom Restoration Act unconstitutional as applied to actions of state and local governments.

These guidelines continue to reflect two basic and equally important obligations imposed on public school officials by the First Amendment. First, schools may not forbid students acting on their own from expressing their personal religious views or beliefs solely because they are of a religious nature. Schools may not discriminate against private religious expression by students, but must instead give students the same right to engage in religious activity and discussion as they have to engage in other comparable activity. Generally, this means that students may pray in a non-disruptive manner during the school day when they are not engaged in school activities and instruction, subject to the same rules of order that apply to other student speech.

At the same time, schools may not endorse religious activity or doctrine, nor may they coerce participation in religious activity. Among other things, of course, school administrators and teachers may not organize or encourage prayer exercises in the classroom. Teachers, coaches and other school officials who act as advisors to student groups must remain mindful that they cannot engage in or lead the religious activities of students.

And the right of religious expression in school does not include the right to have a "captive audience" listen, or to compel other students to participate. School officials should not permit student religious speech to turn into religious harassment aimed at a student or a small group of students. Students do not have the right to make repeated invitations to other students to participate in religious activity in the face of a request to stop.

The statement of principles set forth below derives from the First Amendment. Implementation of these principles, of course, will depend on specific factual contexts and will require careful consideration in particular cases.

In issuing these revised guidelines I encourage every school district to make sure that principals, teachers, students and parents are familiar with their content. To that end I offer three suggestions:

First, school districts should use these guidelines to revise or develop their own district wide policy regarding religious expression. In developing such a policy, school officials can engage parents, teachers, the various faith communities and the broader community in a positive dialogue to define a common ground that gives all parties the assurance that when questions do arise regarding religious expression the community is well prepared to apply these guidelines to specific cases. The Davis County School District in Farmington, Utah, is an example of a school district that has taken the affirmative step of developing such a policy.

At a time of increasing religious diversity in our country such a proactive step can help school districts create a framework of civility that reaffirms and strengthens the community consensus regarding religious liberty. School districts that do not make the effort to develop their own policy may find themselves unprepared for the intensity of the debate that can engage a community when positions harden around a live controversy involving religious expression in public schools.

Second, I encourage principals and administrators to take the additional step of making sure that teachers, so often on the front line of any dispute regarding religious expression, are fully informed about the guidelines. The Gwinnett County School system in Georgia, for example, begins every school year with workshops for teachers that include the distribution of these presidential guidelines. Our nation's schools of education can also do their part by ensuring that prospective teachers are knowledgeable about religious expression in the classroom.

Third, I encourage schools to actively take steps to inform parents and students about religious expression in school using these guidelines. The Carter County School District in Elizabethton, Tennessee, included the subject of religious expression in a character education program that it developed in the fall of 1997. This effort included sending home to every parent a copy of the "Parent's Guide to Religion in the Public Schools."

Help is available for those school districts that seek to develop policies on religious expression. I have enclosed a list of associations and groups that can provide information to school districts and parents who seek to learn more about religious expression in our nation's public schools.

In addition, citizens can turn to the U.S. Department of Education web site (http://www.ed.gov) for information about the guidelines and other activities of the Department that support the growing effort of educators and religious communities to support the education of our nation's children.

Finally, I encourage teachers and principals to see the First Amendment as something more than a piece of dry, old parchment locked away in the national attic gathering dust. It is a vital living principle, a call to action, and a demand that each generation reaffirm its connection to the basic idea that is America — that we are a free people who protect our freedoms by respecting the freedom of others who differ from us.

Our history as a nation reflects the history of the Puritan, the Quaker, the Baptist, the Catholic, the Jew and many others fleeing persecution to find religious freedom in America. The United States remains the most successful experiment in religious freedom that the world has ever known because the First Amendment uniquely balances freedom of private religious belief and expression with freedom from state-imposed religious expression.

Public schools can neither foster religion nor preclude it. Our public schools must treat religion with fairness and respect and vigorously protect religious expression as well as the freedom of conscience of all other students. In so doing our public schools reaffirm the First Amendment and enrich the lives of their students.

I encourage you to share this information widely and in the most appropriate manner with your school community. Please accept my sincere thanks for your continuing work on behalf of all of America's children.

Sincerely,
Richard W. Riley
U.S. Secretary of Education

Presidential Guidelines on Religious Expression in Public Schools
(Revised May 1998)

Student prayer and religious discussion: The Establishment Clause of the First Amendment does not prohibit purely private religious speech by students. Students therefore have the same right to engage in individual or group prayer and religious discussion during the school day as they do to engage in other comparable activity. For example, students may read their Bibles or other scriptures, say grace before meals, and pray before tests to the same extent they may engage in comparable non-disruptive activities. Local school authorities possess substantial discretion to impose rules of order and other pedagogical restrictions on student activities, but they may not structure or administer such rules to discriminate against religious activity or speech.

Generally, students may pray in a non-disruptive manner when not engaged in school activities or instruction, and subject to the rules that normally pertain in the applicable setting. Specifically, students in informal settings, such as cafeterias and hallways, may pray and discuss their religious views with each other, subject to the same rules of order as apply to other student activities and speech. Students may also speak to, and attempt to persuade, their peers about religious topics just as they do with regard to political topics. School officials, however, should intercede to stop student speech that constitutes harassment aimed at a student or a group of students.

Students may also participate in before or after school events with religious content, such as "see you at the flag pole" gatherings, on the same terms as they may participate in other noncurriculum activities on school premises. School officials may neither discourage nor encourage participation in such an event.

The right to engage in voluntary prayer or religious discussion free from discrimination does not include the right to have a captive audience listen, or to compel other students to participate. Teachers and school administrators should ensure that no student is in any way coerced to participate in religious activity.

Graduation prayer and baccalaureates: Under current Supreme Court decisions, school officials may not mandate or organize prayer at graduation, nor organize religious baccalaureate ceremonies. If a school generally opens its facilities to private groups, it must make its facilities available on the same terms to organizers of privately sponsored religious baccalaureate services. A school may not extend preferential treatment to baccalaureate ceremonies and may in some instances be obliged to disclaim official endorsement of such ceremonies.

Official neutrality regarding religious activity: Teachers and school administrators, when acting in those capacities, are representatives of the state and are prohibited by the establishment clause from soliciting or encouraging religious activity, and from participating in such activity with students. Teachers and administrators also are prohibited from discouraging activity because of its religious content, and from soliciting or encouraging antireligious activity.

Teaching about religion: Public schools may not provide religious instruction, but they may teach about religion, including the Bible or other scripture: the history of religion, comparative religion, the Bible (or other scripture)-as-literature, and the role of religion in the history of the United States and other countries all are permissible public school subjects. Similarly, it is permissible to consider religious influences on art, music, literature, and social studies. Although public schools may teach about religious holidays, including their religious aspects, and may celebrate the secular aspects of holidays, schools may not observe holidays as religious events or promote such observance by students.

Student assignments: Students may express their beliefs about religion in the form of homework, artwork, and other written and oral assignments free of discrimination based on the religious content of their submissions. Such home and classroom work should be judged by ordinary academic standards of substance and relevance, and against other legitimate pedagogical concerns identified by the school.

Religious literature: Students have a right to distribute religious literature to their schoolmates on the same terms as they are permitted to distribute other literature that is unrelated to school curriculum or activities. Schools may impose the same reasonable time, place, and manner or other constitutional restrictions on distribution of religious literature as they do on nonschool literature generally, but they may not single out religious literature for special regulation.

Religious excusals: Subject to applicable State laws, schools enjoy substantial discretion to excuse individual students from lessons that are objectionable to the student or the students' parents on religious or other conscientious grounds. However, students generally do not have a Federal right to be excused from lessons that may be inconsistent with their religious beliefs or practices. School officials may neither encourage nor discourage students from availing themselves of an excusal option.

Released time: Subject to applicable State laws, schools have the discretion to dismiss students to off-premises religious instruction, provided that schools do not encourage or discourage participation or penalize those who do not attend. Schools may not allow religious instruction by outsiders on school premises during the school day.

Teaching values: Though schools must be neutral with respect to religion, they may play an active role with respect to teaching civic values and virtue, and the moral code that holds us together as a community. The fact that some of these values are held also by religions does not make it unlawful to teach them in school.

Student garb: Schools enjoy substantial discretion in adopting policies relating to student dress and school uniforms. Students generally have no Federal right to be exempted from religiously-neutral and generally applicable school dress rules based on their religious beliefs or practices; however, schools may not single out religious attire in general, or attire of a particular religion, for prohibition or regulation. Students may display religious messages on items of clothing to the same extent that they are permitted to display other comparable messages. Religious messages may not be singled out for suppression, but rather are subject to the same rules as generally apply to comparable messages.

The Equal Access Act

The Equal Access Act is designed to ensure that, consistent with the First Amendment, student religious activities are accorded the same access to public school facilities as are student secular activities. Based on decisions of the Federal courts, as well as its interpretations of the Act, the Department of Justice has advised that the Act should be interpreted as providing, among other things, that:

General provisions: Student religious groups at public secondary schools have the same right of access to school facilities as is enjoyed by other comparable student groups. Under the Equal Access Act, a school receiving Federal funds that allows one or more student noncurriculum-related clubs to meet on its premises during noninstructional time may not refuse access to student religious groups.

Prayer services and worship exercises covered: A meeting, as defined and protected by the Equal Access Act, may include a prayer service, Bible reading, or other worship exercise.

Equal access to means of publicizing meetings: A school receiving Federal funds must allow student groups meeting under the Act to use the school media—including the public address system, the school newspaper, and the school bulletin board—to announce their meetings on the same terms as other noncurriculum-related student groups are allowed to use the school media. Any policy concerning the use of school media must be applied to all noncurriculum-related student groups in a nondiscriminatory matter. Schools, however, may inform students that certain groups are not school sponsored.

Lunch-time and recess covered: A school creates a limited open forum under the Equal Access Act, triggering equal access rights for religious groups, when it allows students to meet during their lunch periods or other noninstructional time during the school day, as well as when it allows students to meet before and after the school day.

Secretary's Letter on Constitutionally Protected Prayer in Public Elementary and Secondary Schools

February 7, 2003

Dear Colleague:

As part of the implementation of the No Child Left Behind Act of 2001 (NCLB), I am issuing guidance today on constitutionally protected prayer in public elementary and secondary schools. The purpose of this guidance is to provide State educational agencies (SEAs), local educational agencies (LEAs) and the public with information on this important topic. The guidance also sets forth and explains the responsibilities of SEAs and LEAs with respect to this aspect of the NCLB Act. Most significantly, as a condition of receiving funds under the Elementary and Secondary Education Act (ESEA), an LEA must certify in writing to its SEA that it has no policy that prevents, or otherwise denies participation in, constitutionally protected prayer in public schools as set forth in this guidance.

The guidance clarifies the rights of students to pray in public schools. As stated in the guidance, "...the First Amendment forbids religious activity that is sponsored by the government but protects religious activity that is initiated by private individuals" such as students. Therefore, "[a]mong other things, students may read their Bibles or other scriptures, say grace before meals, and pray or study religious materials with fellow students during recess, the lunch hour, or other noninstructional time to the same extent that they may engage in nonreligious activities." Public schools should not be hostile to the religious rights of their students and their families.

At the same time, school officials may not "compel students to participate in prayer or other religious activities." Nor may teachers, school administrators and other school employees, when acting in their official capacities as representatives of the state, encourage or discourage prayer, or participate in such activities with students.

In these challenging times, it is more important than ever to recognize the freedoms we have. I hope that this guidance can contribute to a common understanding of the meaning of the First Amendment in the public school setting. I encourage you to distribute this guidance widely in your community and to discuss its contents and importance with school administrators, teachers, parents, and students.

Sincerely,

Secretary Rod Paige
United States Department of Education

Guidance on Constitutionally Protected Prayer in Public Elementary and Secondary Schools

February 7, 2003

Introduction

Section 9524 of the Elementary and Secondary Education Act ("ESEA") of 1965, as amended by the No Child Left Behind Act of 2001, requires the Secretary to issue guidance on constitutionally protected prayer in public elementary and secondary schools. In addition, Section 9524 requires that, as a condition of receiving ESEA funds, a local educational agency ("LEA") must certify in writing to its State educational agency ("SEA") that it has no policy that prevents, or otherwise denies participation in, constitutionally protected prayer in public schools as set forth in this guidance.

The purpose of this guidance is to provide SEAs, LEAs, and the public with information on the current state of the law concerning constitutionally protected prayer in the public schools, and thus to clarify the extent to which prayer in public schools is legally protected. This guidance also sets forth the responsibilities of SEAs and LEAs with respect to Section 9524 of the ESEA. As required by the Act, this guidance has been jointly approved by the Office of the General Counsel in the Department of Education and the Office of Legal Counsel in the Department of Justice as reflecting the current state of the law. It will be made available on the Internet through the Department of Education's web site (www.ed.gov). The guidance will be updated on a biannual basis, beginning in September 2004, and provided to SEAs, LEAs, and the public.

The Section 9524 Certification Process

In order to receive funds under the ESEA, an LEA must certify in writing to its SEA that no policy of the LEA prevents, or otherwise denies participation in, constitutionally protected prayer in public elementary and secondary schools as set forth in this guidance. An LEA must provide this certification to the SEA by October 1, 2002, and by October 1 of each subsequent year during which the LEA participates in an ESEA program. However, as a transitional matter, given the timing of this guidance, the initial certification must be provided by an LEA to the SEA by March 15, 2003.

The SEA should establish a process by which LEAs may provide the necessary certification. There is no specific Federal form that an LEA must use in providing this certification to its SEA. The certification may be provided as part of the application process for ESEA programs, or separately, and in whatever form the SEA finds most appropriate, as long as the certification is in writing and clearly states that the LEA has no policy that prevents, or otherwise denies participation in, constitutionally protected prayer in public elementary and secondary schools as set forth in this guidance.

By November 1 of each year, starting in 2002, the SEA must send to the Secretary a list of those LEAs that have not filed the required certification or against which complaints have been made to the SEA that the LEA is not in compliance with this guidance. However, as a transitional matter, given the timing of this guidance, the list otherwise due November 1, 2002, must be sent to the Secretary by April 15, 2003. This list should be sent to:

Office of Elementary and Secondary Education
Attention: (Jeanette Lim)
U.S. Department of Education
400 Maryland Avenue, S.W.

Washington, D.C. 20202

The SEA's submission should describe what investigation or enforcement action the SEA has initiated with respect to each listed LEA and the status of the investigation or action. The SEA should not send the LEA certifications to the Secretary, but should maintain these records in accordance with its usual records retention policy.

Enforcement of Section 9524

LEAs are required to file the certification as a condition of receiving funds under the ESEA. If an LEA fails to file the required certification, or files it in bad faith, the SEA should ensure compliance in accordance with its regular enforcement procedures. The Secretary considers an LEA to have filed a certification in bad faith if the LEA files the certification even though it has a policy that prevents, or otherwise denies participation in, constitutionally protected prayer in public elementary and secondary schools as set forth in this guidance.

The General Education Provisions Act ("GEPA") authorizes the Secretary to bring enforcement actions against recipients of Federal education funds that are not in compliance with the law. Such measures may include withholding funds until the recipient comes into compliance. Section 9524 provides the Secretary with specific authority to issue and enforce orders with respect to an LEA that fails to provide the required certification to its SEA or files the certification in bad faith.

Overview of Governing Constitutional Principles

The relationship between religion and government in the United States is governed by the First Amendment to the Constitution, which both prevents the government from establishing religion and protects privately initiated religious expression and activities from government interference and discrimination.[1] The First Amendment thus establishes certain limits on the conduct of public school officials as it relates to religious activity, including prayer.

The legal rules that govern the issue of constitutionally protected prayer in the public schools are similar to those that govern religious expression generally. Thus, in discussing the operation of Section 9524 of the ESEA, this guidance sometimes speaks in terms of "religious expression." There are a variety of issues relating to religion in the public schools, however, that this guidance is not intended to address.

The Supreme Court has repeatedly held that the First Amendment requires public school officials to be neutral in their treatment of religion, showing neither favoritism toward nor hostility against religious expression such as prayer.[2] Accordingly, the First Amendment forbids religious activity that is sponsored by the government but protects religious activity that is initiated by private individuals, and the line between government-sponsored and privately initiated religious expression is vital to a proper understanding of the First Amendment's scope. As the Court has explained in several cases, "there is a crucial difference between government speech endorsing religion, which the Establishment Clause forbids, and private speech endorsing religion, which the Free Speech and Free Exercise Clauses protect."[3]

The Supreme Court's decisions over the past forty years set forth principles that distinguish impermissible governmental religious speech from the constitutionally protected private religious speech of students. For example, teachers and other public school officials may not lead their classes in prayer, devotional readings from the Bible, or other religious activities.[4] Nor may school officials attempt to persuade or compel students to participate in prayer or other religious activities.[5] Such conduct is "attributable to the State" and thus violates the Establishment Clause.[6]

Similarly, public school officials may not themselves decide that prayer should be included in school-sponsored events. In Lee v. Weisman[7], for example, the Supreme Court held that public school officials violated the Constitution in inviting a member of the clergy to deliver a prayer at a graduation ceremony. Nor may school officials grant religious speakers preferential access to public audiences, or otherwise select public speakers on a basis that favors religious speech. In Santa Fe Independent School District v. Doe[8], for example, the Court invalidated a school's football game speaker policy on the ground that it was designed by school officials to result in pre-game prayer, thus favoring religious expression over secular expression.

Although the Constitution forbids public school officials from directing or favoring prayer, students do not "shed their constitutional rights to freedom of speech or expression at the schoolhouse gate,"[9] and the Supreme Court has made clear that "private religious speech, far from being a First Amendment orphan, is as fully protected under the Free Speech Clause as secular private expression."[10] Moreover, not all religious speech that takes place in the public schools or at school-sponsored events is governmental speech.[11] For example, "nothing in the Constitution ... prohibits any public school student from voluntarily praying at any time before, during, or after the schoolday,"[12] and students may pray with fellow students during the school day on the same terms and conditions that they may engage in other conversation or speech. Likewise, local school authorities possess substantial discretion to impose rules of order and pedagogical restrictions on student activities,[13] but they may not structure or administer such rules to discriminate against student prayer or religious speech. For instance, where schools permit student expression on the basis of genuinely neutral criteria and students retain primary control over the content of their expression, the speech of students who choose to express themselves through religious means such as prayer is not attributable to the state and therefore may not be restricted because of its religious content.[14] Student remarks are not attributable to the state simply because they are delivered in a public setting or to a public audience.[15] As the Supreme Court has explained: "The proposition that schools do not endorse everything they fail to censor is not complicated,"[16] and the Constitution mandates neutrality rather than hostility toward privately initiated religious expression.[17]

Prayer During Non-Instructional Time

Students may pray when not engaged in school activities or instruction, subject to the same rules designed to prevent material disruption of the educational program that are applied to other privately initiated expressive activities. Among other things, students may read their Bibles or other scriptures, say grace before meals, and pray or study religious materials with fellow students during recess, the lunch hour, or other non-instructional time to the same extent that they may engage in nonreligious activities. While school authorities may impose rules of order and pedagogical restrictions on student activities, they may not discriminate against student prayer or religious speech in applying such rules and restrictions.

Organized Prayer Groups and Activities

Students may organize prayer groups, religious clubs, and "see you at the pole" gatherings before school to the same extent that students are permitted to organize other non-curricular student activities groups. Such groups must be given the same access to school facilities for assembling as is given to other non-curricular groups, without discrimination because of the religious content of their expression. School authorities possess substantial discretion concerning whether to permit the use of school media for student advertising or announcements regarding non-curricular activities. However, where student groups that meet for nonreligious activities are permitted to advertise or announce their meetings—for example, by advertising in a student newspaper, making announcements on a student activities bulletin board or public address system, or handing out leaflets—school authorities may not discriminate against groups who meet to pray. School authorities may disclaim sponsorship of non-curricular groups and events, provided they administer such disclaimers in a manner that neither favors nor disfavors groups that meet to engage in prayer or religious speech.

Teachers, Administrators, and other School Employees

When acting in their official capacities as representatives of the state, teachers, school administrators, and other school employees are prohibited by the Establishment Clause from encouraging or discouraging prayer, and from actively participating in such activity with students. Teachers may, however, take part in religious activities where the overall context makes clear that they are not participating in their official capacities. Before school or during lunch, for example, teachers may meet with other teachers for prayer or Bible study to the same extent that they may engage in other conversation or nonreligious activities. Similarly, teachers may participate in their personal capacities in privately sponsored baccalaureate ceremonies.

Moments of Silence

If a school has a "minute of silence" or other quiet periods during the school day, students are free to pray silently, or not to pray, during these periods of time. Teachers and other school employees may neither encourage nor discourage students from praying during such time periods.

Accommodation of Prayer During Instructional Time

It has long been established that schools have the discretion to dismiss students to off-premises religious instruction, provided that schools do not encourage or discourage participation in such instruction or penalize students for attending or not attending. Similarly, schools may excuse students from class to remove a significant burden on their religious exercise, where doing so would not impose material burdens on other students. For example, it would be lawful for schools to excuse Muslim students briefly from class to enable them to fulfill their religious obligations to pray during Ramadan.

Where school officials have a practice of excusing students from class on the basis of parents' requests for accommodation of nonreligious needs, religiously motivated requests for excusal may not be accorded less favorable treatment. In addition, in some circumstances, based on federal or state constitutional law or pursuant to state statutes, schools may be required to make accommodations that relieve substantial burdens on students' religious exercise. Schools officials are therefore encouraged to consult with their attorneys regarding such obligations.

Religious Expression and Prayer in Class Assignments

Students may express their beliefs about religion in homework, artwork, and other written and oral assignments free from discrimination based on the religious content of their submissions. Such home and classroom work should be judged by ordinary academic standards of substance and relevance and against other legitimate pedagogical concerns identified by the school. Thus, if a teacher's assignment involves writing a poem, the work of a student who submits a poem in the form of a prayer (for example, a psalm) should be judged on the basis of academic standards (such as literary quality) and neither penalized nor rewarded on account of its religious content.

Student Assemblies and Extracurricular Events

Student speakers at student assemblies and extracurricular activities such as sporting events may not be selected on a basis that either favors or disfavors religious speech. Where student speakers are selected on the basis of genuinely neutral, evenhanded criteria and retain primary control over the content of their expression, that expression is not attributable to the school and therefore may not be restricted because of its religious (or anti-religious) content. By contrast, where school officials determine or substantially control the content of what is expressed, such speech is attributable to the school and may not include prayer or other specifically religious (or anti-religious) content. To avoid any mistaken perception that a school endorses student speech that is not in fact attributable to the school, school officials may make appropriate, neutral disclaimers to clarify that such speech (whether religious or nonreligious) is the speaker's and not the school's.

Prayer at Graduation

School officials may not mandate or organize prayer at graduation or select speakers for such events in a manner that favors religious speech such as prayer. Where students or other private graduation speakers are selected on the basis of genuinely neutral, evenhanded criteria and retain control over the content of their expression, however, that expression is not attributable to the school and therefore may not be restricted because of its religious (or anti-religious) content. To avoid any mistaken perception that a school endorses student or other private speech that is not in fact attributable to the school, school officials may make appropriate, neutral disclaimers to clarify that such speech (whether religious or nonreligious) is the speaker's and not the school's.

Baccalaureate Ceremonies

School officials may not mandate or organize religious ceremonies. However, if a school makes its facilities and related services available to other private groups, it must make its facilities and services available on the same terms to organizers of privately sponsored religious baccalaureate ceremonies. In addition, a school may disclaim official endorsement of events sponsored by private groups, provided it does so in a manner that neither favors nor disfavors groups that meet to engage in prayer or religious speech.

Notes:

[1] The relevant portions of the First Amendment provide: "Congress shall make no law respecting an establishment of religion or prohibiting the free exercise thereof; or abridging the freedom of speech . . . ." U.S. Const. amend. I. The Supreme Court has held that the Fourteenth Amendment makes these provisions applicable to all levels of government—federal, state, and local—and to all types of governmental policies and activities. See Everson v. Board of Educ., 330 U.S. 1 (1947); Cantwell v. Connecticut, 310 U.S. 296 (1940).

[2] See, e.g., Everson, 330 U.S. at 18 (the First Amendment "requires the state to be a neutral in its relations with groups of religious believers and non-believers; it does not require the state to be their adversary. State power is no more to be used so as

to handicap religions than it is to favor them"); Good News Club v. Milford Cent. Sch., 533 U.S. 98 (2001).

[3] Santa Fe Indep. Sch. Dist. v. Doe, 530 U.S. 290, 302 (2000) (quoting Board of Educ. v. Mergens, 496 U.S. 226, 250 (1990) (plurality opinion)); accord Rosenberger v. Rector of Univ. of Virginia, 515 U.S. 819, 841 (1995).

[4] Engel v. Vitale, 370 U.S. 421 (1962) (invalidating state laws directing the use of prayer in public schools); School Dist. of Abington Twp. v. Schempp, 374 U.S. 203 (1963) (invalidating state laws and policies requiring public schools to begin the school day with Bible readings and prayer); Mergens, 496 U.S. at 252 (plurality opinion) (explaining that "a school may not itself lead or direct a religious club"). The Supreme Court has also held, however, that the study of the Bible or of religion, when presented objectively as part of a secular program of education (e.g., in history or literature classes), is consistent with the First Amendment. See Schempp, 374 U.S. at 225.

[5] See Lee v. Weisman, 505 U.S. 577, 599 (1992); see also Wallace v. Jaffree, 472 U.S. 38 (1985).

[6] See Weisman, 505 U.S. at 587.

[7] 505 U.S. 577 (1992).

[8] 530 U.S. 290 (2000).

[9] Tinker v. Des Moines Indep. Community Sch. Dist., 393 U.S. 503, 506 (1969).

[10] Capitol Square Review & Advisory Bd. v. Pinette, 515 U.S. 753, 760 (1995).

[11] Santa Fe, 530 U.S. at 302 (explaining that "not every message" that is "authorized by a government policy and take[s] place on government property at government-sponsored school-related events" is "the government's own").

[12] Santa Fe, 530 U.S. at 313.

[13] For example, the First Amendment permits public school officials to review student speeches for vulgarity, lewdness, or sexually explicit language. Bethel Sch. Dist. v. Fraser, 478 U.S. 675, 683-86 (1986). Without more, however, such review does not make student speech attributable to the state.

[14] Rosenberger v. Rector of Univ. of Virginia, 515 U.S. 819 (1995); Board of Educ. v. Mergens, 496 U.S. 226 (1990); Good News Club v. Milford Cent. Sch., 533 U.S.

98 (2001); Lamb's Chapel v. Center Moriches Union Free Sch. Dist., 508 U.S. 384 (1993); Widmar v. Vincent, 454 U.S. 263 (1981); Santa Fe, 530 U.S. at 304 n.15. In addition, in circumstances where students are entitled to pray, public schools may not restrict or censor their prayers on the ground that they might be deemed "too religious" to others. The Establishment Clause prohibits state officials from making judgments about what constitutes an appropriate prayer, and from favoring or disfavoring certain types of prayers—be they "nonsectarian" and "nonproselytizing" or the opposite—over others. See Engel v. Vitale, 370 U.S. 421, 429-30 (1962) (explaining that "one of the greatest dangers to the freedom of the individual to worship in his own way lay in the Government's placing its official stamp of approval upon one particular kind of prayer or one particular form of religious services," that "neither the power nor the prestige" of state officials may "be used to control, support or influence the kinds of prayer the American people can say," and that the state is "without power to prescribe by law any particular form of prayer"); Weisman, 505 U.S. at 594.

[15] Santa Fe, 530 U.S. at 302; Mergens, 496 U.S. at 248-50.

[16] Mergens, 496 U.S. at 250 (plurality opinion); id. at 260-61 (Kennedy, J., concurring in part and in judgment).

[17] Rosenberger, 515 U.S. at 845-46; Mergens, 496 U.S. at 248 (plurality opinion); id. at 260-61 (Kennedy, J., concurring in part and in judgment).

Equal Access Act 20 U.S.C. § 4071.
Denial of equal access prohibited

(a) Restriction of limited open forum on basis of religious, political, philosophical, or other speech content prohibited

It shall be unlawful for any public secondary school which receives Federal financial assistance and which has a limited open forum to deny equal access or a fair opportunity to, or discriminate against, any students who wish to conduct a meeting within that limited open forum on the basis of the religious, political, philosophical, or other content of the speech at such meetings.

(b) "Limited open forum" defined

A public secondary school has a limited open forum whenever such school grants an offering to or opportunity for one or more noncurriculum related student groups to meet on school premises during noninstructional time.

(c) Fair opportunity criteria

Schools shall be deemed to offer a fair opportunity to students who wish to conduct a meeting within its limited open forum if such school uniformly provides that—

(1) the meeting is voluntary and student-initiated;
(2) there is no sponsorship of the meeting by the school, the government, or its agents or employees;
(3) employees or agents of the school or government are present at religious meetings only in a nonparticipatory capacity;
(4) the meeting does not materially and substantially interfere with the orderly conduct of educational activities within the school; and
(5) nonschool persons may not direct, conduct, control, or regularly attend activities of student groups.

(d) Construction of subchapter with respect to certain rights

Nothing in this subchapter shall be construed to authorize the United States or any State or political subdivision thereof—

(1) to influence the form or content of any prayer or other religious activity;

(2) to require any person to participate in prayer or other religious activity;

(3) to expend public funds beyond the incidental cost of providing the space for student-initiated meetings;

(4) to compel any school agent or employee to attend a school meeting if the content of the speech at the meeting is contrary to the beliefs of the agent or employee;

(5) to sanction meetings that are otherwise unlawful;

(6) to limit the rights of groups of students which are not of a specified numerical size; or

(7) to abridge the constitutional rights of any person.

(e) Federal financial assistance to schools unaffected

Notwithstanding the availability of any other remedy under the Constitution or the laws of the United States, nothing in this subchapter shall be construed to authorize the United States to deny or withhold Federal financial assistance to any school.

(f) Authority of schools with respect to order, discipline, well-being, and attendance concerns

Nothing in this subchapter shall be construed to limit the authority of the school, its agents or employees, to maintain order and discipline on school premises, to protect the well-being of students and faculty, and to assure that attendance of students at meetings is voluntary.

20 U.S.C. § 4072. Definitions

As used in this subchapter—

(1) The term "secondary school" means a public school which provides secondary education as determined by State law.

(2) The term "sponsorship" includes the act of promoting, leading, or participating in a meeting. The assignment of a teacher, administrator, or other school employee to a meeting for custodial purposes does not constitute sponsorship of the meeting.
(3) The term "meeting" includes those activities of student groups which are permitted under a school's limited open forum and are not directly related to the school curriculum.
(4) The term "noninstructional time" means time set aside by the school before actual classroom instruction begins or after actual classroom instruction ends.

CONCERNING TEACHERS, SCHOOL STAFF, AND OFFICIALS

Under current law, public school teachers, staff, and officials have First Amendment free speech and free exercise rights only with respect to other school personnel, not with respect to students. Teachers, as agents of the state in a government school, are prohibited by current Supreme Court Establishment Clause legal analysis (often popularly referred to as "the doctrine of the separation of church and state") from sharing their religious beliefs with students. However, teachers continue to have free speech and free exercise rights as employees within their government-operated workplace (the school). These rights include the right to engage in religious expression with other employees of the school. Religious exchanges between school employees, however, should always take place out of sight of students.

> *Teachers, as agents of the state in a government school, are prohibited by current Supreme Court Establishment Clause legal analysis from sharing their religious beliefs with students.*

Teachers are considered to be agents of the government when they are present on the school campus, engaging in school activities, and interacting with students. Therefore, anything they say regarding religion is attributable to the government and can be a violation of the First Amendment Establishment Clause, which prohibits an establishment of religion by the government (which courts now interpret to require a complete "separation of church and state").

Given this relatively new legal climate, many teachers and other school personnel are unclear about how much of their faith they can share with students. Christian teachers who have been teaching for many years are often perplexed when typical interactions they have had for years with students about religion are now suddenly declared to be unconstitutional. When they are reprimanded by their superiors in the school system, they are often shocked to discover that they have done something wrong.

While courts have said that neither teachers nor students

lose their constitutional rights at the schoolhouse door, students are permitted a great deal more religious liberty in public school than are teachers or other school officials.

In today's America, a teacher in public school is considered to be an agent of the government rather than of the parent.

While teachers in America were originally presumed to be agents (or extensions or representatives) of the parents, that situation changed in the mid-20th Century as courts began to permit the government to exert more and more control over schools. In today's America, a teacher in public school is considered to be an agent (or extension or representative) of the government rather than of the parent. As a representative of the state, a teacher must remain totally religion-neutral with students in school or risk a legal reprimand for violation of the First Amendment Establishment Clause, which courts say does not permit the government to favor one religion over others.

These legal restrictions on teacher-student interactions about religion are a double-edged sword for parents. Communities are no longer uniformly Christian, and many public school teachers are no longer Christians. The religious beliefs of some students will always be compromised if teachers or other school personnel are permitted to promote their own faith with their students.

Ultimately, all education is religious at its core, however. When Christianity is no longer the dominant faith in school, the result is that other religions or no religion will be the message given to students. That is one reason why many Christian parents believe so strongly that, whenever possible, families should make every effort to educate their children in a Christian environment.

On the other hand, the many Christian teachers who feel called to public schools to reach students who receive no religious training at home must also be supported and encouraged. Such dedicated servants of God must learn to successfully navigate the turbulent waters of current legal requirements for public school teachers.

The following questions are those that are most often asked by public school teachers and other school staff and officials.

What free speech and free exercise rights do teachers still retain in public schools?

The United States Supreme Court has held that neither students nor teachers shed their constitutional rights (including their free speech and free exercise rights) at the schoolhouse door. However, as applied to school staff and teachers, courts have only upheld these rights in public schools with respect to other school personnel, not to teacher communications with students. Just as in other government workplaces, the school may control a teacher's speech in front of students (who are the "customers" or "clients" of the government's education business). Courts have determined that Establishment Clause considerations generally trump a teacher's free speech and free exercise rights when the two conflict. Since the teacher is an agent of the government while on school property or engaging in school activities, anything the teacher says concerning religion can be attributed to the government and can become an unconstitutional establishment of religion.

When teachers communicate with other employees, however, they enjoy all of the free exercise rights of other government employees as controlled by the legal principles described in the Religious Guidelines for Federal Employees, included in this section.

May teachers communicate with other school personnel about religion either in conversations or in writing?

Teachers have the right while in school to express themselves to fellow employees as long as such communication takes place in the faculty room or otherwise out of hearing of students. The Establishment Clause is not violated when school personnel communicate between themselves about religion; it can only be violated when they communicate improperly with students about religion. Teachers who share religious convictions may always have private conversations about religion with other employees or pray together so long as students are not included and cannot overhear their conversation or prayers.

Teachers must use this free expression right wisely, being careful not to express themselves to other employees who do not welcome such religious interaction. As in all workplaces, once a fellow-employee tells another employee that his religious communication is unwelcome, any continued religious communication with that employee could be considered harassment. If a teacher's religious expression with other employees becomes substantially disruptive to the work environment, he could also be prohibited from such religious expression. All school staff, including bus drivers and cafeteria workers, have the same rights and restrictions as teachers with regard to students and to other employees.

May teachers include religious references in correspondence with parents of students?

If a teacher is corresponding with the parent in her capacity as the student's teacher, school officials may prohibit the use of religious references. Since the school is permitted to control communications between teachers and parents, the teacher should abide by such instructions and omit any religious references. On the other hand, if the teacher is certain that such references would be welcome by the parent and her school superiors have not prohibited it, the teacher should use her best judgment and her knowledge of the student and his family to determine whether to include religious references in parent communications. Of course, outside the school environment, such as at church or at non-school activities, teachers and parents may communicate freely.

May teachers post inspirational messages from the Bible on faculty only bulletin boards?

It would be viewpoint discrimination in violation of First Amendment rights of free speech if other school personnel were permitted to display items of general interest or encouragement on a faculty bulletin board, but religious messages were prohibited. The only exception to this general legal principle would be if the bulletin board were in a location where it was visible to students. However, school officials may neutrally declare a bulletin board off-limits for all but school-related items.

Similarly, if there is a place not visible to students where teachers are free to leave reading material to share with others, religious material may not be singled out for prohibition. If other teachers do not want to read religious material, they are free to leave it alone.

May teachers hold faculty Bible studies or prayer groups in public schools?

As government employees, teachers are free to practice their faith at appropriate times while on the job. Because of Establishment Clause concerns, however, teachers may not exercise this right with or in the presence of students. Teachers who wish to pray or engage in other group religious activities must do so outside the presence of students.

Teachers have free speech rights to conduct their own prayer and Bible study with their fellow teachers when away from their students. Such free speech rights may be exercised only when no students are present. Teachers and school staff must be permitted to form prayer and Bible study groups among themselves and use the faculty room for such a meeting if other groups are permitted to organize and use the faculty room (or other location) for non-religious, non-work related gatherings. In fact, the school would be interfering with the free speech rights of the teachers if it prohibited them from meeting together for this purpose merely because their activity was religious. The United States Supreme Court has held that prayer and other types of religious activity are a form of free speech protected by the Constitution.

Teachers who wish to pray or engage in other group religious activities must do so outside the presence of students.

Teachers should be careful not to draw the attention of students to such religiously oriented meetings. Finally, if a teacher or other supervisory personnel participate in the meeting, they must be careful to let other subordinate employees know that their participation or lack of participation in the religious meetings will not affect their job with respect to hiring, promotion, or termination.

May teachers keep a personal Bible or other religious material on their desk?

A teacher may not keep a personal Bible or other religious objects on her desk if they are not being used as part of an objective and neutral academic curriculum. The teacher may also be prohibited from reading a Bible during free reading times in the classroom while students are present. Courts have ruled that a teacher would violate the Establishment Clause by this overt expression of a particular religion. However, the teacher could keep a personal Bible in her desk drawer or in some other location out of sight of the students and could read the Bible during times when students are not present in the classroom.

> *A teacher may not keep a personal Bible or other religious materials on her desk if they are not being used as part of an objective and neutral academic curriculum.*

Teachers may not keep Bibles in a classroom library unless the Bibles are included with other religious texts (such as the Koran) as a small part of a general classroom library the students may consult for academic purposes. Similarly, a teacher should not display religious material in the classroom unless it is directly related to the curriculum and is not either devotional or proselytizing in nature.

May teachers wear religious clothing or jewelry in the classroom?

In contrast to a student's nearly universal right to wear religious jewelry or clothing with religious messages in school, a teacher is more limited, particularly with respect to clothing choices. Generally, a school district may prohibit a teacher from wearing religious garb or clothing with religious messages in order to promote an atmosphere of neutrality about religion in the public school classroom. On the other hand, teachers may be permitted to wear such religious jewelry as cross necklaces or angel pins in the classroom. A general rule would be that if a jewelry item can be purchased at a department store jewelry counter, it may be worn since its use would not then be limited to religious purposes. Many "rock" stars who are not Christians like to wear cross jewelry on stage, for instance.

May teachers who object to political or anti-religious positions taken by teachers' unions withhold that portion of their union dues?

Public employee unions may only require a pro rata share of dues to be used for legitimate costs of union benefits, such as collective bargaining. If an employee (including a teacher) objects to dues being spent on political or ideological causes, that employee has a free speech right not to be compelled to support that portion of union activities. Teachers must be permitted to redirect that portion of their union dues that would be used to support objectionable ideological or political causes to an alternate organization. Generally, that choice must be approved by the union. Teachers may also elect to join an alternative teacher's organization.

May teachers pray privately with students outside of class?

Teachers should not pray with students in school. If a teacher believes a student needs prayer or if a student directly asks the teacher to pray for him, the teacher should arrange to meet the student away from the school campus. The student's parent should be notified that the teacher intends to respond to the student in this manner and should be asked to give consent. The teacher could meet with the student for such a purpose at a church or at a neutral location such as a fast food restaurant near the school property.

Teachers have been fired for praying with students in school. For example, in one case where a close friend of a student had died and the student requested prayer after class, the teacher was fired for accommodating the student's request and praying with her. Another teacher was fired because she encouraged her elementary school students to pray on their own before going to lunch. If fired for praying with a student at school, the teacher would have no legal recourse.

In considering the appropriateness of praying with students in school, consider the matter turned upside-down. Place yourself in the role of a parent with a child in the public school. Imagine that your child approached a teacher who practiced the Wiccan religion and asked the teacher to cast a spell on her behalf. Would you be concerned if the school permitted such interaction without your express consent?

May teachers give their personal viewpoint in answer to a student's questions about religion?

Teachers are always permitted to teach about religion or to answer students' questions (either in or out of class) about religion as long as they do so in an objective, neutral, and academic manner. Such religious interchanges with students must always be age-appropriate and must be for pedagogical rather than for proselytizing purposes. When engaging in such academic discussions, students should not be able to discern the personal faith of the teacher. Even questions about salvation may be answered in an objective manner that does not indicate that the teacher shares that belief.

While it seems logical that teachers should be permitted to discuss their own personal viewpoints (including their religious viewpoints) with students both inside and outside the classroom, the law has moved in the past few decades in a different direction that considers such sharing to be an unconstitutional government imposition (or establishment) of a particular religion.

This movement in the law can, therefore, be interpreted to mean that while teachers may have opportunities to share their religious viewpoints during class time or during private conversations with students, teachers do not have a right to do so. If a teacher knows her students, their families, the community, the school board, and her superiors well, and knows for a certainty that such sharing about personal religious viewpoints would be universally welcome, it is probably not risky to engage in such sharing. On the other hand, if any of these variables might not support such sharing about religion, doing so could be a risky undertaking for the teacher. A teacher must be willing to risk losing her job if she engages in such personal sharing about her faith with students.

> *If there is no school policy and there are no complaints, principals have a great deal of discretion as to what they will permit teachers to do in the classroom with respect to religion.*

Generally, problems arise when either students or parents complain to school administrators about personal religious exchanges between teachers and students. A teacher would likely have no legal recourse if fired for sharing personal religious viewpoints with students, particularly in violation of a specific controlling school policy. If there is no school policy and there are no complaints, principals have a great deal of discretion as to what they will permit teachers to do in the classroom with respect to religion.

May teachers interact with students regarding religion while away from the school campus?

Teacher do not forfeit their right to engage in religious activities on their own time, away from the school campus. Teachers may not be prohibited from attending church, even if one or more of their students attend the same church. Away from the school, teachers may attend religious activities with their students, may lead their students to Christ, or teach them in a Sunday school class, at which time the teacher is free to discuss all religious matters with them, including devotionals and proselytizing. Teachers may also serve as church youth leaders outside of school time, even if a teacher's own students are part of the youth group. When a teacher is not actually on campus or on contract time for the school, the restrictions of the Establishment Clause do not apply.

While teachers may not invite students during contract time

to attend church or other religious activities, teachers may contact a student's parents on their own time to invite the student or parent to church, such as during a door-to-door church visitation program. The teacher should make clear that the invitation is being extended on a personal level and not in any capacity as the child's teacher. The teacher should also make clear that the parent's or child's reaction to the invitation (whether positive or negative) will have no bearing on the teacher's interaction with the student in class. Anytime teachers interact with students on a religious level away from school, they should make certain the student understands the teacher is not acting as a representative of the school, but is acting as a private individual. Teachers need to be very careful, however, even when engaging in such interaction away from school since some courts have said that a school may prohibit such interaction, particularly if contact information is obtained from school files.

May teachers talk about their personal religious viewpoints in the classroom?

In general, teachers may not read the Bible or tell Bible stories, conduct devotional exercises, or pray in the classroom. Teachers should not witness to students even in private conversation while on school grounds unless they are certain that school administrators would permit such conversations. On the other hand, teachers may always include objective information about religion wherever it naturally falls in the course curriculum. Generally, the safest way for teachers and students to interact subjectively about religious issues is off campus after the teacher's workday has ended and the student's parents have given permission for the exchange.

Occasionally, a specific situation demonstrates why teachers are not permitted to proselytize their students during school hours. One father called our office concerned that his daughter was being forced to participate in non-Christian religious observances prior to the Christmas holidays. Since the school had banned the celebration of Christmas, this first grade teacher had decided to have her public school class engage in activities surrounding her own celebration of

Kwanzaa. The teacher believed that Kwanzaa was purely a cultural and not a religious holiday, but our attorneys were able to demonstrate to school officials that students were, in fact, being exposed to pagan religious rituals during these holiday celebrations. School officials intervened to prevent this religious activity in class.

Another father called when his second grader was required to participate in an art project in which the students made Buddhist worship artifacts. The students were then taken to a Buddhist Temple to observe how the Buddhist priests used these objects in worship. The elementary school principal was shocked that a Christian parent would not want his child to participate in this "cultural" field trip. Our attorneys pointed out to the principal that he would not likely have permitted this second grade teacher to take the class to a Catholic mass or to a Baptist revival service or require the students to make crucifixes in art class. The Buddhist trip was no different.

A mother called when her daughter was taught that the Bible was no more inspired than the Koran. This teacher had also informed her students that Catholicism was the only true religion. Generally, parents do not want their children exposed to proselytizing in school by religious groups with which they do not agree. Therefore, Christian teachers are also prohibited from engaging in Christian witnessing activities with students in class.

When a teacher's superior instructs her not to discuss her personal religious viewpoints in the classroom, that request should be diligently adhered to. Some teachers have legally been fired, not for discussing religion specifically, but for disobeying the direct order of a superior.

On the other hand, if no school policy forbids it, if administrators would not object and if a teacher knows her class well enough to discuss her personal religious viewpoints in the classroom, the following guidelines should be strictly adhered to:

1. The discussion should be relevant to the academic curriculum.
2. The comments should be age-appropriate.
3. The discussion should not take up a large percentage of classroom time.

4. The teacher should make sure that students understand these are her personal viewpoints, which the students are free to either accept or reject, and that they do not represent the view of the school district.
5. The teacher should be careful not to engage in any sort of proselytizing in the classroom—either for or against religion.

The guidelines given above should only be followed in circumstances where the teacher has never been told by the administration to avoid discussing religion in the classroom. A teacher may also choose to answer questions about her personal religious viewpoint by engaging in a two-part answer. The teacher could say: "A Christian believes" and then follow-up that comment, if asked, by telling the class that she is a Christian. Even this type of exchange should be avoided, however, if the teacher has already been told not to discuss religion with students.

A good teacher will not want to offend the religious sensitivities of any child in her classroom.

In the absence of complaints by students or parents, teachers and other school officials have a great deal of discretion as to what will be permitted in the classroom. Teachers are generally free to control the content of their classroom discussions, including religious content, subject only to directives by principals or other school officials. Teachers should always make themselves aware of the range of religious beliefs (or non-belief) that exists in their classes and should make decisions about religion accordingly. A good teacher will not want to offend the religious sensitivities of any child in her classroom.

May teachers permit students to discuss religion in the classroom?

Since students do have freedom of speech in school, they should be permitted to discuss their personal religious beliefs in the classroom as long as their comments are pertinent to the discussion at hand. Since the teacher exercises pedagogical control of the classroom, she must permit students to discuss religion when it is relevant to the topic at hand. However, all religious viewpoints should be equally welcomed and the teacher's religious viewpoint should not be obvious.

May teachers participate in student Bible clubs?

The Equal Access Act does not permit teachers to participate in the substantive religious discussions of a student religious club. The clubs must be both student-initiated and student-led. A teacher assigned by the school to attend meetings of an Equal Access Bible Club may attend only in a non-participatory capacity under the specific terms of the EAA, which is printed in the student section of this resource.

A faculty member may meet with student leaders of the Bible club off campus in order to assist and train them to witness to other students. One teacher who contacted us about this matter was initially frustrated by this restriction, but chose to use the situation to mentor a few student leaders and train them to disciple other students. It was heartening for this teacher to then see the students take an active role in leading their classmates to Christ, something that might not have developed so well had the students relied on the teacher to do the witnessing herself.

> *A faculty member may meet with student leaders of the Bible club off campus in order to assist and train them to witness to other students.*

Schools may appoint non-religious, or even anti-religious, teachers to monitor the Bible club. This situation can even have a positive result. One student reported to our office that his Bible club's school-appointed monitor accepted Christ as her Savior when the student gave a salvation invitation to the other students. While this response may have technically violated the Establishment Clause, none of the club's students complained about the experience to school officials.

May teachers participate in student-initiated and student-led prayer activities such as "See You At the Pole"?

It is clear that neither school officials nor teachers may encourage or discourage student participation in student-initiated and student-led prayer events such as SYATP. It is also clear that the school may appoint a teacher or several teachers to monitor such student events. In such cases, however, the monitor should not become a participant. Since events such as SYATP are generally permitted under the Equal Access Act, it is reasonable to assume that the same restrictions would apply with respect to participation by teachers or school officials in the prayer.

What is less clear is how the courts would apply the rules to a teacher attending and participating in a SYATP event as a private citizen if the event occurred before the official start of the school day. A teacher should not attend and participate, even under these circumstances, if she was specifically told not to do so by her superiors. If school officials have not specifically prohibited teacher participation, however, it is legally unclear as to whether teachers who have not started their workday could attend and participate.

It is less risky legally for teachers who have already started their work day to meet together with other teachers for prayer at another location (perhaps in the faculty lounge) during the SYATP event to avoid the appearance of school sponsorship, while still supporting the students in prayer.

May coaches lead sports teams in prayer before games?

Many coaches are unclear about their right to pray with students before a sporting event. Since courts have held this practice to be unconstitutional, our attorneys recommend that coaches absent themselves from pre-game prayers and permit the students to initiate and lead the prayers on their own. If coaches are present, they may take a respectful posture, but should not actively participate in the student prayers.

Although the constitutionality of this approach has never been tested in court, according to general rules regarding Establishment Clause principles, one way for a coach to participate in a voluntary prayer time might be to gather with the players off school property before he and the players are required to be at the school. For example, one community little league coach told players on his team that he would be praying at a picnic table adjacent to the official playing field 15 minutes before he was scheduled to be at the field. Any players who wanted to join him for prayer at that time, before their scheduled game time, were free to do so. Another coach invited his players to attend various churches with him on their own time on Sunday mornings. Invitations for such activities should be extended away from the school and with parental knowledge and approval.

May a school bus driver, cafeteria worker, janitor, or secretary talk to students about religion or pray with them?

All school staff and employees, including bus drivers and other staff, are under the same restrictions as teachers with respect to religious interaction with students. Bus drivers and other staff are also agents of the state and, therefore, capable of violating the Establishment Clause.

However, just as with teachers, when bus drivers or other school personnel are away from the school and on their own time, they may interact with students about religion.

Several other situations may arise with bus drivers. For instance, a bus driver is generally not permitted to play religious music on the bus or to have a Bible visible on the bus while students are on board. However, a bus driver could permit students to take turns choosing a radio station and religious students could be permitted to choose a religious station when their turn came. Also, bus drivers should permit students to interact privately with each other regarding religion while on the bus, as long as the interaction does not cause disruption or constitute harassment.

Key Cases Impacting Rights of Teachers in Public Schools

Cases Involving Teacher Interaction with Other School Personnel

Tinker v. Des Moines Indep. Community Sch. Dist., 393 U.S. 503 (1969).

This is the key case supporting free speech rights for both students and teachers in public schools. The Supreme Court plainly declared: "It can hardly be argued that either students or teachers shed their constitutional rights to freedom of speech or expression at the schoolhouse gate." While courts have limited this right with respect to teacher/student interaction, teachers generally have free speech rights to express themselves freely, even about religion, to other teachers while on school property, subject only to prohibition of harassment.

Widmar v. Vincent, 545 U.S. 263 (1981).

The United States Supreme Court has held that prayer and other forms of religious activity are a form of free speech protected by the Constitution.

May v. Evansville-Vanderburg Sch. Corp., 787 F.2d 1105 (7th Cir. 1986).

A court upheld the school district's prohibition of a prayer and worship meeting that several teachers were conducting prior to the start of the school day and before students arrived at school. In this case, the teachers could not show that the school had permitted any other non-school related teachers meetings for any purpose, either religious or secular. If other meetings had been permitted, this case would likely have had a different resolution.

Cases Involving Teachers' Unions

Abood v. Detroit Bd. of Educ., 431 U.S. 209 (1977).

Public employees, including teachers, have a free speech right not to be compelled to support political or ideological speech by unions with which they do not agree. Actually, this is a First Amendment right not to speak.

Chicago Teachers v. Hudson, 475 U.S. 292 (1986).

Teachers unions must offer teachers a way to avoid compulsory union contributions for ideological purposes. Teachers must be permitted to redirect that portion of their union dues that will not be used for collective bargaining purposes but will support causes or ideas with which the teacher disagrees.

Lehnert v. Ferris Faculty Association, 500 U.S. 507 (1990).

A union may not charge for lobbying, but may require teachers to contribute a pro rata share of dues used for costs of union benefits.

Cases Involving Religious Speech by Teachers in the Classroom

Everson v. Board of Education, 330 U.S. 1 (1947).

The United States Supreme Court held that the religion clauses, including the Establishment Clause of the First Amendment, applied to individual states through the Due Process Clause of the Fourteenth Amendment. This led to prohibition of religious speech by school officials, who are agents of the government. The Court also said that the Establishment Clause of the First Amendment "requires the state to be a neutral in its relations with . . . religious believers and non-believers; it does not require the state to be their adversary." Also, "State power is no more to be used to handicap religions, than it is to favor them."

Palmer v. Chicago Bd. of Educ., 603 F.2d 1271 (7th Cir. 1979).

A probationary kindergarten teacher was dismissed when she refused to teach patriotic songs or explain national holidays to the children because she claimed that her religious beliefs would be violated. The court held that she did not have a right to refuse to teach these curriculum subjects. However, the court said the school could not compel her to participate in the pledge of allegiance against her religious beliefs.

Breen v. Runkel, 614 F. Supp. 355 (S.D. Mich. 1985).

Teachers have no constitutional right to pray in their classrooms, read from the Bible, or tell stories that have a Biblical basis. However, school administrators are not required to ban all religion from the classroom.

Hazelwood v. Kuhlmeier, 484 U.S. 260 (1988).

Generally, the school administration or school board has ultimate authority to determine what materials must be included in, or deleted from, the curriculum. Teachers do not have academic freedom or free speech rights to deviate from school policies regarding curriculum once they have been set in place. However, where no specific policy exists, teachers have more freedom over their classroom curriculum.

Webster v. New Lenox, 917 F.2d 1004 (7th Cir. 1990).

The school board has the authority to forbid the teaching of non-evolutionary theories of origin. Note that such a policy is not required, however.

Roberts v. Madigan, 921 F.2d 1047 (10th Cir. 1990), cert. denied, 505 U.S. 1218 (1991).

The court upheld a principal's order that a teacher remove his personal Bible from his desk, where it was visible to students, and that he not read it during free reading time when students were present in the classroom. The school implied that the teacher was using these privileges to proselytize students. The court held that teachers may not share their faith with students while performing their professional duties. Note that this policy is not required.

United States v. Board of Education, 911 F.2d 882 (3rd Cir. 1990).

The court ruled that a school district could prohibit teachers from wearing religious garb in order to preserve the appearance of religious neutrality in the classroom.

Bishop v. Aronox, 926 F.2d 1066 (11th Cir. 1991), cert. denied, 505 U.S. 1218 (1992).

The court held that a university could direct an assistant professor not to discuss his religious viewpoints in the classroom.

Peloza v. Capistrano Unified Sch. Dist., 37 F.3d 517 (9th Cir. 1994).

A teacher was fired for teaching his personal religious views about evolution to his students. The court held that permitting a teacher "to discuss his religious beliefs with students during school time on school grounds would violate the Establishment Clause of the First Amendment."

Helland v. South Bend Comm. Sch. Corp., 93 F.3d 327 (7th Cir. 1996).

A school may direct a teacher not to discuss her religious viewpoints in the classroom or other school settings. In this case, a substitute teacher was fired without recourse for reading the Bible and distributing religious material to students in class. Several other courts have also upheld such bans. Another possible implication of this line of cases would be that if teachers are not required by a supervisor to withhold discussion of religious viewpoints in class, they may be permitted. If a teacher does choose to comment about religion in the classroom, however, the guidelines should be considered. Such comments should ----

1. Be relevant to the subject at hand.
2. Be appropriate for the age level of students in the class.
3. Not take up a disproportionate amount of class time.
4. Be prefaced with a disclaimer that these are her personal views and do not represent the views of the school district.
5. Only be in response to a student question.

However, if requested by a superior to curtail any expression of religion in the classroom, the teacher should comply. In general, students should not be aware of their teacher's religious affiliation or lack thereof, even when religious topics are discussed as part of the academic curriculum.

Marchi v. BOCES, 173 F.3d 469 (2d Cir. 1999).

A teacher was terminated after discussing his religious beliefs at length in class for several years.

Downs v. Los Angeles Unified School Dist., 228 F.3d 1003 (9th Cir. 2000).

Posters on a hallway bulletin board promoting gay and lesbian awareness week were representing the message of the local government through the school board. Since they were government speech, the school could deny the right of a teacher to post an opposing viewpoint on the board.

Downing v. West Haven Board of Ed., 162 F.Supp.2d 19 (D.Conn. 2001).

A school had the authority to insist that a teacher cover her tee shirt displaying the words "Jesus 2000" in four-inch letters during instructional hours. The court noted: "[P]ublic school officials have the authority to prevent teachers from giving students and others the impression that the school prefers a particular religion, or religion in general. 'Thus, schools may direct teachers to refrain from expression of religious viewpoints in the classroom and like settings; indeed, schools have a constitutional duty to make certain that subsidized teachers do not inculcate religion.'

Williams v. Vidmar, 367 F.Supp.2d 1265 (N.D.Cal. 2005).

Teachers do not have a First Amendment right to determine what curriculum will be taught in the classroom. They do, however, have the right to be treated the same way other teachers are, regardless of religion.

Lee v. York County Sch. Dist., 484 F.3d 687 (4th Cir. 2007).

A high school teacher sued the school when schools officials received complaints and removed religious postings from his classroom bulletin board, including news items about the National Day of Prayer and President Bush's religious beliefs. The court ruled that the teacher's free speech rights were not violated because "courts have generally recognized that public schools possess the right to regulate speech that occurs within a compulsory classroom setting." The court ruled that schools are not public forums where free speech rights are protected and that teachers do not have unbridled free speech rights during the school day. Note, however, that school officials are not required to impose such restrictive policies.

Doe v. Duncanville Indep. Sch. Dist., 70 F.3d 402 (5th Cir. 1995).

A coach may not actively pray with his team before a game because such conduct would be an establishment of religion even if the students had initiated the prayer. However, the coach could exercise deference or respect during any student-initiated prayers before a game.

Braswell v. Board of Regents of University System of Georgia, 369 F.Supp.2d 1362 (N.D.Ga. 2005).

A university cheerleading coach was reprimanded and placed on probation after a team member complained that she injected religion in her coaching, prayed with the team, and favored Christian members over non-Christians. The coach sued and the court determined that the school was within its rights to respond to the student's complaint as it did. Note that such policies are not required.

Cases Involving Teacher Participation in Student Religious Activities

Board of Educ. v. Mergens, 496 U.S. 226 (1990).

In response to numerous complaints that public schools were discriminating against student religious clubs, the United States Congress passed the Equal Access Act ("EAA") in 1984. The Act is included in the student section. The Court ruled that a school may not prohibit or deny equal access to student Bible clubs when other non-curriculum-related student groups are permitted to meet. However, teachers may only participate in student Bible clubs in a supervisory capacity.

Daugherty v. Vanguard Charter Academy, 116 F. Supp. 2d 897 (W.D. Mich. 2000).

The court held that teachers could be present at SYATP events as long as their presence was one of "custodial oversight" and "merely to ensure order and good behavior." (*Quoting, Board of Educ. of Westside Community Schools v. Mergens*, 496 U.S. 226, 253 (1990)).

Sease v. Sch. Dist. of Philadelphia, 811 F. Supp. 183 (E.D. Pa. 1993).

The Equal Access Act does not permit a school employee to participate in a student religious club, and the employee does not have a free speech right to participate.

Quappe v. Endry, 772 F. Supp. 1004 (S.D. Ohio 1991), aff'd., 979 F.2d 851 (6th Cir. 1992).

The court prohibited the club meetings of elementary school students immediately after school because a teacher was heavily involved in leading the meeting and in recruiting students to attend.
Wigg v. Sioux Falls School Dist. 49-5, 382 F.3d 807 (8th Cir. 2004).
A school could not bar a teacher from attending an after-school Bible club even at her own school because she was acting as a private citizen on her own time.

THE WHITE HOUSE
Office of the Press Secretary

For Immediate Release, August 14, 1997

Guidelines on Religious Exercise and Religious Expression in the Federal Workplace

The following Guidelines, addressing religious exercise and religious expression, shall apply to all civilian executive branch agencies, officials, and employees in the Federal workplace.

These Guidelines principally address employees' religious exercise and religious expression when the employees are acting in their personal capacity within the Federal workplace and the public does not have regular exposure to the workplace. The Guidelines do not comprehensively address whether and when the government and its employees may engage in religious speech directed at the public. They also do not address religious exercise and religious expression by uniformed military personnel, or the conduct of business by chaplains employed by the Federal Government. Nor do the Guidelines define the rights and responsibilities of nongovernmental employers including religious employers — and their employees. Although these Guidelines, including the examples cited in them, should answer the most frequently encountered questions in the Federal workplace, actual cases sometimes will be complicated by additional facts and circumstances that may require a different result from the one the Guidelines indicate.

Section 1. Guidelines for Religious Exercise and Religious Expression in the Federal Workplace.

Executive departments and agencies ("agencies") shall permit personal religious expression by Federal employees to the greatest extent possible, consistent with requirements of law and interests in workplace efficiency as described in this set of Guidelines. Agencies shall not discriminate against employees on the basis of religion, require religious participation or nonparticipation as a condition of employment, or permit religious harassment. And agencies shall accommodate employees' exercise of their religion in the circumstances specified in these Guidelines. These requirements are but applications of the general principle that agencies shall treat all employees with the same respect and consideration, regardless of their religion (or lack thereof).

A. Religious Expression. As a matter of law, agencies shall not restrict personal religious expression by employees in the Federal workplace except where the employee's interest in the expression is outweighed by the government's interest in the efficient provision of public services or where the expression intrudes upon the legitimate rights of other employees or creates the appearance, to a reasonable observer, of an official endorsement of religion. The examples cited in these Guidelines as permissible forms of religious expression will rarely, if ever, fall within these exceptions.

As a general rule, agencies may not regulate employees' personal religious expression on the basis of its content or viewpoint. In other words, agencies generally may not suppress employees' private religious speech in the workplace while leaving unregulated other private employee speech that has a comparable effect on the efficiency of the workplace — including ideological speech on politics and other topics — because to do so would be to engage in presumptively unlawful content or viewpoint discrimination. Agencies, however, may, in their discretion, reasonably regulate the time, place and manner of all employee speech, provided such regulations do not discriminate on the basis of content or viewpoint.

The Federal Government generally has the authority to regulate an employee's private speech, including religious speech, where the employee's interest in that speech is outweighed by the government's interest in promoting the efficiency of the public services it performs. Agencies should exercise this authority evenhandedly and with restraint, and with regard for the fact that Americans are used to expressions of disagreement on controversial subjects, including religious ones. Agencies are not required, however, to permit employees to use work time to pursue religious or ideological agendas. Federal employees are paid to perform official work, not to engage in personal religious or ideological campaigns during work hours.

(1) Expression in Private Work Areas. Employees should be permitted to engage in private religious expression in personal work areas not regularly open to the public to the same extent that they may engage in non-religious private expression, subject to reasonable content and viewpoint-neutral standards and restrictions: such religious expression must be permitted as long as it does not interfere with the agency's carrying out of its official responsibilities.

Examples

(a) An employee may keep a Bible or Koran on her private desk and read it during breaks.

(b) An agency may restrict all posters, or posters of a certain size, in private work areas, or require that such posters be displayed facing the employee, and not on common walls; but the employer typically cannot single out religious or anti-religious posters for harsher or preferential treatment.

(2) Expression Among Fellow Employees. Employees should be permitted to engage in religious expression with fellow employees, to the same extent that they may engage in comparable nonreligious private expression, subject to reasonable and content-neutral standards and restrictions: such expression should not be restricted as long as it does not interfere with workplace efficiency. Though agencies are entitled to regulate such employee speech based on reasonable predictions of disruption, they should not restrict speech based on merely hypothetical concerns, having little basis in fact, that the speech will have a deleterious effect on workplace efficiency.

Examples

(a) In informal settings, such as cafeterias and hallways, employees are entitled to discuss their religious views with one another, subject only to the same rules of order as apply to other employee expression. If an agency permits unrestricted nonreligious expression of a controversial nature, it must likewise permit equally controversial religious expression.

(b) Employees are entitled to display religious messages on items of clothing to the same extent that they are permitted to display other comparable messages. As long as they do not convey any governmental endorsement of religion, religious messages may not typically be singled out for suppression.

(c) Employees generally may wear religious medallions over their clothes or so that they are otherwise visible. Typically, this alone will not affect workplace efficiency, and therefore is protected.

(3) Expression Directed at Fellow Employees. Employees are permitted to engage in religious expression directed at fellow employees, and may even attempt to persuade fellow employees of the correctness of their religious views, to the same extent as those employees may engage in comparable speech not involving religion. Some religions encourage adherents to spread the faith at every opportunity, a duty that can encompass the adherent's workplace. As a general matter, proselytizing is as entitled to constitutional protection as any other form of speech — as long as a reasonable observer would not interpret the expression as government endorsement of religion. Employees may urge a colleague to participate or not to participate in religious activities to the same extent that, consistent with concerns of workplace efficiency, they may urge their colleagues to engage in or refrain from other personal endeavors. But employees must refrain from such expression when a fellow employee asks that it stop or otherwise demonstrates that it is unwelcome. (Such expression by supervisors is subject to special consideration as discussed in Section B(2) of these guidelines.)

Examples

(a) During a coffee break, one employee engages another in a polite discussion of why his faith should be embraced. The other employee disagrees with the first employee's religious exhortations, but does not ask that the conversation stop. Under these circumstances, agencies should not restrict or interfere with such speech.

(b) One employee invites another employee to attend worship services at her church, though she knows that the invitee is a devout adherent of another faith. The invitee is shocked, and asks that the invitation not be repeated. The original invitation is protected, but the employee should honor the request that no further invitations be issued.

(c) In a parking lot, a non-supervisory employee hands another employee a religious tract urging that she convert to another religion lest she be condemned to eternal damnation. The proselytizing employee says nothing further and does not inquire of his colleague whether she followed the pamphlet's urging. This speech typically should not be restricted.

Though personal religious expression such as that described in these examples, standing alone, is protected in the same way, and to the same extent, as other constitutionally valued speech in the Federal workplace, such expression should not be permitted if it is part of a larger pattern of verbal attacks on fellow employees (or a specific employee) not sharing the faith of the speaker. Such speech, by virtue of its excessive or harassing nature, may constitute religious harassment or create a hostile work environment, as described in Part B(3) of these Guidelines, and an agency should not tolerate it.

(4) Expression in Areas Accessible to the Public. Where the public has access to the Federal workplace, all Federal employers must be sensitive to the Establishment Clause's requirement that expression not create the reasonable impression that the government is sponsoring, endorsing, or inhibiting religion generally, or favoring or disfavoring a particular religion. This is particularly important in agencies with ad judicatory functions.

However, even in workplaces open to the public, not all private employee religious expression is forbidden. For example, Federal employees may wear personal religious jewelry absent special circumstances (such as safety concerns) that might require a ban on all similar nonreligious jewelry. Employees may also display religious art and literature in their personal work areas to the same extent that they may display other art and literature, as long as the viewing public would reasonably understand the religious expression to be that of the employee acting in her personal capacity, and not that of the government itself. Similarly, in their private time employees may discuss religion with willing coworkers in public spaces to the same extent as they may discuss other subjects, as long as the public would reasonably understand the religious expression to be that of the employees acting in their personal capacities.

B. Religious Discrimination. Federal agencies may not discriminate against employees on the basis of their religion, religious beliefs, or views concerning religion.

(1) Discrimination in Terms and Conditions. No agency within the executive branch may promote, refuse to promote, hire, refuse to hire, or otherwise favor or disfavor, an employee or potential employee because of his or her religion, religious beliefs, or views concerning religion.

Examples

(a) A Federal agency may not refuse to hire Buddhists, or impose more onerous requirements on applicants for employment who are Buddhists.

(b) An agency may not impose, explicitly or implicitly, stricter promotion requirements for Christians, or impose stricter discipline on Jews than on other employees, based on their religion. Nor may Federal agencies give advantages to Christians in promotions, or impose lesser discipline on Jews than on other employees based on their religion.

(c) A supervisor may not impose more onerous work requirements on an employee who is an atheist because that employee does not share the supervisor's religious beliefs.

(2) Coercion of Employee's Participation or Nonparticipation in Religious Activities. A person holding supervisory authority over an employee may not, explicitly or implicitly, insist that the employee participate in religious activities as a condition of continued employ-

ment, promotion, salary increases, preferred job assignments, or any other incidents of employment. Nor may a supervisor insist that an employee refrain from participating in religious activities outside the workplace except pursuant to otherwise legal, neutral restrictions that apply to employees' off-duty conduct and expression in general (e.g., restrictions on political activities prohibited by the Hatch Act).

This prohibition leaves supervisors free to engage in some kinds of speech about religion. Where a supervisor's religious expression is not coercive and is understood as his or her personal view, that expression is protected in the Federal workplace in the same way and to the same extent as other constitutionally valued speech. For example, if surrounding circumstances indicate that the expression is merely the personal view of the supervisor and that employees are free to reject or ignore the supervisor's point of view or invitation without any harm to their careers or professional lives, such expression is so protected.

Because supervisors have the power to hire, fire, or promote, employees may reasonably perceive their supervisors' religious expression as coercive, even if it was not intended as such. Therefore, supervisors should be careful to ensure that their statements and actions are such that employees do not perceive any coercion of religious or nonreligious behavior (or respond as if such coercion is occurring), and should, where necessary, take appropriate steps to dispel such misperceptions.

Examples

(a) A supervisor may invite coworkers to a son's confirmation in a church, a daughter's bat mitzvah in a synagogue, or to his own wedding at a temple. But a supervisor should not say to an employee: "I didn't see you in church this week. I expect to see you there this Sunday."

(b) On a bulletin board on which personal notices unrelated to work regularly are permitted, a supervisor may post a flyer announcing an Easter musical service at her church, with a handwritten notice inviting coworkers to attend. But a supervisor should not circulate a memo announcing that he will be leading a lunch hour Talmud class that employees should attend in order to participate in a discussion of career advancement that will convene at the conclusion of the class.

(c) During a wide-ranging discussion in the cafeteria about various non-work related matters, a supervisor states to an employee her belief that religion is important in one's life. Without more, this is not coercive, and the statement is protected in the Federal workplace in the same way, and to the same extent, as other constitutionally valued speech.

(d) A supervisor who is an atheist has made it known that he thinks that anyone who attends church regularly should not be trusted with the public weal. Over a period of years, the supervisor regularly awards merit increases to employees who do not attend church routinely, but not to employees of equal merit who do attend church. This course of conduct would reasonably be perceived as coercive and should be prohibited.

(e) At a lunch table discussion about abortion, during which a wide range of views are vigorously expressed, a supervisor shares with those he supervises his belief that God demands full respect for unborn life, and that he believes it is appropriate for all persons to pray for the unborn. Another supervisor expresses the view that abortion should be kept legal because God teaches that women must have control over their own bodies. Without more, neither of these comments coerces employees' religious conformity or conduct. Therefore, unless the supervisors take further steps to coerce agreement with their view or act in ways that could reasonably be perceived as coercive, their expressions are protected in the Federal workplace in the same way and to the same extent as other constitutionally valued speech.

(3) Hostile Work Environment and Harassment. The law against workplace discrimination protects Federal employees from being subjected to a hostile environment, or religious harassment, in the form of religiously discriminatory intimidation, or pervasive or se-

vere religious ridicule or insult, whether by supervisors or fellow workers. Whether particular conduct gives rise to a hostile environment, or constitutes impermissible religious harassment, will usually depend upon its frequency or repetitiveness, as well as its severity. The use of derogatory language in an assaultive manner can constitute statutory religious harassment if it is severe or invoked repeatedly. A single incident, if sufficiently abusive, might also constitute statutory harassment. However, although employees should always be guided by general principles of civility and workplace efficiency, a hostile environment is not created by the bare expression of speech with which some employees might disagree. In a country where freedom of speech and religion are guaranteed, citizens should expect to be exposed to ideas with which they disagree.

The examples below are intended to provide guidance on when conduct or words constitute religious harassment that should not be tolerated in the Federal workplace. In a particular case, the question of employer liability would require consideration of additional factors, including the extent to which the agency was aware of the harassment and the actions the agency took to address it.

Examples

(a) An employee repeatedly makes derogatory remarks to other employees with whom she is assigned to work about their faith or lack of faith. This typically will constitute religious harassment. An agency should not tolerate such conduct.

(b) A group of employees subjects a fellow employee to a barrage of comments about his sex life, knowing that the targeted employee would be discomforted and offended by such comments because of his religious beliefs. This typically will constitute harassment, and an agency should not tolerate it.

(c) A group of employees that share a common faith decides that they want to work exclusively with people who share their views. They engage in a pattern of verbal attacks on other employees who do not share their views, calling them heathens, sinners, and the like. This conduct should not be tolerated.

(d) Two employees have an angry exchange of words. In the heat of the moment, one makes a derogatory comment about the other's religion. When tempers cool, no more is said. Unless the words are sufficiently severe or pervasive to alter the conditions of the insulted employee's employment or create an abusive working environment, this is not statutory religious harassment.

(e) Employees wear religious jewelry and medallions over their clothes or so that they are otherwise visible. Others wear buttons with a generalized religious or anti-religious message. Typically, these expressions are personal and do not alone constitute religious harassment.

(f) In her private work area, a Federal worker keeps a Bible or Koran on her private desk and reads it during breaks. Another employee displays a picture of Jesus and the text of the Lord's Prayer in her private work area. This conduct, without more, is not religious harassment, and does not create an impermissible hostile environment with respect to employees who do not share those religious views, even if they are upset or offended by the conduct.

(g) During lunch, certain employees gather on their own time for prayer and Bible study in an empty conference room that employees are generally free to use on a first-come, first-served basis. Such a gathering does not constitute religious harassment even if other employees with different views on how to pray might feel excluded or ask that the group be disbanded.

C. Accommodation of Religious Exercise. Federal law requires an agency to accommodate employees' exercise of their religion unless such accommodation would impose an undue hardship on the conduct of the agency's operations. Though an agency need not make an accommodation that will result in more than a de minimis cost to the agency, that cost or hardship nevertheless must be real rather than speculative or hypothetical: the accommodation should be made unless it would cause an actual cost to the agency or to other employees or an actual disruption of work, or unless it is otherwise barred by law.

In addition, religious accommodation cannot be disfavored vis-à-vis other, nonreligious accommodations. Therefore, a religious accommodation cannot be denied if the agency regularly permits similar accommodations for nonreligious purposes.

Examples

(a) An agency must adjust work schedules to accommodate an employee's religious observance — for example, Sabbath or religious holiday observance — if an adequate substitute is available, or if the employee's absence would not otherwise impose an undue burden on the agency.

(b) An employee must be permitted to wear religious garb, such as a crucifix, a yarmulke, or a head scarf or hijab, if wearing such attire during the work day is part of the employee's religious practice or expression, as long as the wearing of such garb does not unduly interfere with the functioning of the workplace.

(c) An employee should be excused from a particular assignment if performance of that assignment would contravene the employee's religious beliefs and the agency would not suffer undue hardship in reassigning the employee to another detail.

(d) During lunch, certain employees gather on their own time for prayer and Bible study in an empty conference room that employees are generally free to use on a first-come, first-served basis. Such a gathering may not be subject to discriminatory restrictions because of its religious content.

In those cases where an agency's work rule imposes a substantial burden on a particular employee's exercise of religion, the agency must go further: an agency should grant the employee an exemption from that rule, unless the agency has a compelling interest in denying the exemption and there is no less restrictive means of furthering that interest.

Examples

(a) A corrections officer whose religion compels him or her to wear long hair should be granted an exemption from an otherwise generally applicable hair length policy unless denial of an exemption is the least restrictive means of preserving safety, security, discipline or other compelling interests.

(b) An applicant for employment in a governmental agency who is a Jehovah's Witness should not be compelled, contrary to her religious beliefs, to take a loyalty oath whose form is religiously objectionable.

D. Establishment of Religion. Supervisors and employees must not engage in activities or expression that a reasonable observer would interpret as Government endorsement or denigration of religion or a particular religion. Activities of employees need not be officially sanctioned in order to violate this principle; if, in all the circumstances, the activities would leave a reasonable observer with the impression that Government was endorsing, sponsoring, or inhibiting religion generally or favoring or disfavoring a particular religion, they are not permissible. Diverse factors, such as the context of the expression or whether official channels of communication are used, are relevant to what a reasonable observer would conclude.

Examples

(a) At the conclusion of each weekly staff meeting and before anyone leaves the room, an employee leads a prayer in which nearly all employees participate. All employees are required to attend the weekly meeting. The supervisor neither explicitly recognizes the prayer as an official function nor explicitly states that no one need participate in the prayer. This course of conduct is not permitted unless under all the circumstances a reasonable observer would conclude that the prayer was not officially endorsed.

(b) At Christmas time, a supervisor places a wreath over the entrance to the office's main reception area. This course of conduct is permitted.

Section 2. Guiding Legal Principles.

In applying the guidance set forth in section I of this order, executive branch departments and agencies should consider the following legal principles.

A. Religious Expression. It is well-established that the Free Speech Clause of the First Amendment protects Government employees in the workplace. This right encompasses a right to speak about religious subjects. The Free Speech Clause also prohibits the Government from singling out religious expression for disfavored treatment: "[P]rivate religious speech, far from being a First Amendment orphan, is as fully protected under the Free Speech Clause as secular private expression," Capitol Sq. Review Bd. v. Pinette, 115 S.Ct. 2448 (1995). Accordingly, in the Government workplace, employee religious expression cannot be regulated because of its religious character, and such religious speech typically cannot be singled out for harsher treatment than other comparable expression.

Many religions strongly encourage their adherents to spread the faith by persuasion and example at every opportunity, a duty that can extend to the adherents' workplace. As a general matter, proselytizing is entitled to the same constitutional protection as any other form of speech. Therefore, in the governmental workplace, proselytizing should not be singled out because of its content for harsher treatment than nonreligious expression.

However, it is also well-established that the Government in its role as employer has broader discretion to regulate its employees' speech in the workplace than it does to regulate speech among the public at large. Employees' expression on matters of public concern can be regulated if the employees' interest in the speech is outweighed by the interest of the Government, as an employer, in promoting the efficiency of the public services it performs through its employees. Governmental employers also possess substantial discretion to impose content-neutral and viewpoint-neutral time, place, and manner rules regulating private employee expression in the workplace (though they may not structure or administer such rules to discriminate against particular viewpoints). Furthermore, employee speech can be regulated or discouraged if it impairs discipline by superiors, has a detrimental impact on close working relationships for which personal loyalty and confidence are necessary, impedes the performance of the speaker's duties or interferes with the regular operation of the enterprise, or demonstrates that the employee holds views that could lead his employer or the public reasonably to question whether he can perform his duties adequately.

Consistent with its fully protected character, employee religious speech should be treated, within the Federal workplace, like other expression on issues of public concern: in a particular case, an employer can discipline an employee for engaging in speech if the value of the speech is outweighed by the employer's interest in promoting the efficiency of the public services it performs through its employee. Typically, however, the religious speech cited as permissible in the various examples included in these Guidelines will not unduly impede these interests and should not be regulated. And rules regulating employee speech, like other rules regulating speech, must be carefully drawn to avoid any unnecessary limiting or chilling of protected speech.

B. Discrimination in Terms and Conditions. Title VII of the Civil Rights Act of 1964 makes it unlawful for employers, both private and public, to "fail or refuse to hire or to discharge any individual, or otherwise to discriminate against any individual with respect to compensation, terms, conditions, or privileges of employment, because of such individual's ... religion." 42 U.S.C. § 2000e2(a)(l). The Federal Government also is bound by the equal protection component of the Due Process Clause of the Fifth Amendment, which bars intentional discrimination on the basis of religion. Moreover, the prohibition on religious discrimination in employment applies with particular force to the Federal Government, for Article VI, clause 3 of the Constitution bars the Government from enforcing any religious test as a requirement for qualification to any Office. In addition, if a Government law, regulation or practice facially discriminates against employees' private exercise of religion or is intended to infringe upon or restrict private religious exercise, then that law, regulation, or practice implicates the Free Exercise Clause of the First Amendment. Last, under the Religious Freedom Restoration Act, 42 U.S.C. § 2000bb1, Federal governmental action that substantially burdens a private party's exercise of religion can be enforced only if it is justified by a compelling interest and is narrowly tailored to advance that interest.

C. Coercion of Employees' Participation or Nonparticipation in Religious Activities. The ban on religious discrimination is broader than simply guaranteeing nondiscriminatory treatment in formal employment decisions such as hiring and promotion. It applies to all terms and conditions of employment. It follows that the Federal Government may not require or coerce its employees to engage in religious activities or to refrain from engaging in religious activity. For example, a supervisor may not demand attendance at (or a refusal to attend) religious services as a condition of continued employment or promotion, or as a criterion affecting assignment of job duties. Quid pro quo discrimination of this sort is illegal. Indeed, wholly apart from the legal prohibitions against coercion, supervisors may not insist upon employees' conformity to religious behavior in their private lives any more than they can insist on conformity to any other private conduct unrelated to employees' ability to carry out their duties.

D. Hostile Work Environment and Harassment. Employers violate Title VII's ban on discrimination by creating or tolerating a "hostile environment" in which an employee is subject to discriminatory intimidation, ridicule, or insult sufficiently severe or pervasive to alter the conditions of the victim's employment. This statutory standard can be triggered (at the very least) when an employee, because of her or his religion or lack thereof, is exposed to intimidation, ridicule, and insult. The hostile conduct — which may take the form of speech — need not come from supervisors or from the employer. Fellow employees can create a hostile environment through their own words and actions.

The existence of some offensive workplace conduct does not necessarily constitute harassment under Title VII. Occasional and isolated utterances of an epithet that engenders offensive feelings in an employee typically would not affect conditions of employment, and therefore would not in and of itself constitute harassment. A hostile environment, for Title VII purposes, is not created by the bare expression of speech with which one disagrees. For religious harassment to be illegal under Title VII it must be sufficiently severe or pervasive to alter the conditions of employment and create an abusive working environment. Whether conduct can be the predicate for a finding of religious harassment under Title VII depends on the totality of the circumstances, such as the nature of the verbal or physical conduct at issue and the context in which the alleged incidents occurred. As the Supreme Court has said in an analogous context:

[W]hether an environment is "hostile" or "abusive" can be determined only by looking at all the circumstances. These may include the frequency of the discriminatory conduct; its severity; whether it is physically threatening or humiliating, or a mere offensive utterance; and whether it unreasonably interferes with an employee's work performance. The effect on the employee's psychological well-being is, of course, relevant to determining whether the plaintiff actually found the environment abusive. Harris v. Forklift Systems, Inc., 510 U.S. 17 (1993).

The use of derogatory language directed at an employee can rise to the level of religious harassment if it is severe or invoked repeatedly. In particular, repeated religious slurs and negative religious stereotypes, or continued disparagement of an employee's religion or ritual practices, or lack thereof, can constitute harassment. It is not necessary that the harassment be explicitly religious in character or that the slurs reference religion: it is sufficient that the harassment is directed at an employee because of the employee's religion or lack thereof. That is to say, Title VII can be violated by employer tolerance of repeated slurs, insults and/or abuse not explicitly religious in nature if that conduct would not have occurred but for the targeted employee's religious belief or lack of religious belief. Finally although proselytization directed at fellow employees is generally permissible (subject to the special considerations relating to supervisor expression discussed elsewhere in these Guidelines), such activity must stop if the listener asks that it stop[] or otherwise demonstrates that it is unwelcome.

E. Accommodation of Religious Exercise. Title VII requires employers "to reasonably accommodate ... an employee's or prospective employee's religious observance or practice" unless such accommodation would impose an "undue hardship on the conduct of the employer's business." 42 U.S.C. 2000e(j). For example, by statute, if an employee's religious beliefs require her to be absent from work, the Federal Government must grant that employee compensation time for overtime work, to be applied against the time lost, unless to do so would harm the ability of the agency to carry out its mission efficiently. 5 U.S.C. 5550a.

Though an employer need not incur more than de minimis costs in providing an accommodation, the employer hardship nevertheless must be real rather than speculative or hypothetical. Religious accommodation cannot be disfavored relative to other, nonreligious, accommodations. If an employer regularly permits accommodation for nonreligious purposes, it cannot deny comparable religious accommodation: "Such an arrangement would display a discrimination against religious practices that is the antithesis of reasonableness." Ansonia Bd. of Educ. v. Philbrook, 479 U.S. 60, 71 (1986). In the Federal Government workplace, if neutral workplace rules — that is, rules that do not single out religious or religiously motivated conduct for disparate treatment — impose a substantial burden on a particular employee's exercise of religion, the Religious Freedom Restoration Act requires the employer to grant the employee an exemption from that neutral rule, unless the employer has a compelling interest in denying an exemption and there is no less restrictive means of furthering that interest. 42 U.S.C. 2000bb-1

F. Establishment of Religion. The Establishment Clause of the First Amendment prohibits the Government—including its employees—from acting in a manner that would lead a reasonable observer to conclude that the Government is sponsoring, endorsing or inhibiting religion generally or favoring or disfavoring a particular religion. For example, where the public has access to the Federal workplace, employee religious expression should be prohibited where the public reasonably would perceive that the employee is acting in an official, rather than a private, capacity, or under circumstances that would lead a reasonable observer to conclude that the Government is endorsing or disparaging religion. The Establishment Clause also forbids Federal employees from using Government funds or resources (other than those facilities generally available to government employees) for private religious uses.

Section 3. General.

These Guidelines shall govern the internal management of the civilian executive branch. They are not intended to create any new right, benefit, or trust responsibility, substantive or procedural, enforceable at law or equity by a party against the United States, its agencies, its officers, or any person. Questions regarding interpretations of these Guidelines should be brought to the Office of the General Counsel or Legal Counsel in each department and agency.

Historically in America, prayer and religion were part of a student's daily routine in public school. However, this practice dramatically changed in 1962 when the United States Supreme Court decided that official prayer and devotions at the start of the school day would be an unconstitutional establishment of a religion by the government. The Supreme Court had set the stage for this prohibition in 1947 when the Court decided that the First Amendment Establishment Clause (sometimes referred to as "the doctrine of the separation of church and state") applied not only to the federal government, but also to all other governmental entities.

Before 1947, states and local school boards could require prayer and Bible reading without violating the federal Establishment Clause since that Clause did not apply to them. For nearly 200 years after the adoption of the Bill of Rights, its provisions, including the First Amendment, only applied to the federal government, not to other governmental bodies, such as school boards. Since 1947, courts have interpreted the legal doctrine of "the separation of church and state" to prohibit more and more official religious activity in public schools as well as in other public venues.

The following questions are those most often asked concerning curriculum issues in public schools.

Has the Supreme Court prohibited all prayer and Bible reading in public schools?

Actually, the Supreme Court has not totally eliminated prayer or the Bible from public schools; it has only barred school-sponsored religion, including officially led prayers and devotional use of the Bible. According to Supreme Court doctrine developed since the mid-20th Century, the First Amendment to the United States Constitution does not permit officially sponsored prayer or Bible reading in public schools. This does not mean, however, that religion may not continue to be taught in public schools as part of the academic curriculum, as long as the religious instruction is done in a neutral, objective, and academic manner. What constitutes an objective, neutral, and academic use of the Bible will be developed further in this section.

Furthermore, as discussed more fully in the Student section of this book, students continue to have the right to pray individually or in groups or to discuss their religious views with their peers in school as long as they are not disruptive. Because the Establishment Clause does not apply to non-
government private speech, students continue to enjoy the right to read their Bibles or other Scriptures, to say grace before meals, to pray before tests, and to discuss religion privately with others as long as the religious exchange does not constitute harassment of other students.

Religion may be taught in public schools as part of the academic curriculum, as long as the religious instruction is done in a neutral, objective, and academic manner.

Even in the classroom, students have the right to pray quietly on their own at any time. Even courts recognize that the government could not stop students from praying before a test, for instance. In informal settings, such as the cafeteria or hallways, students may pray either audibly or silently, subject to the same rules of order that apply to other speech in these locations. However, the right to engage in voluntary prayer does not include the right to compel other students to participate.

Teachers control the learning environment in their classroom. A teacher must permit students to share religious opinions or information in class discussions or in student assignments where students choose the topics, as long as such sharing is relevant to the assignment or to the topic at hand and as long as the exchange is civil and is not disruptive. Teachers have a great deal of discretion to permit students to enjoy free speech rights with regard to religion while in the classroom. This could include students sharing a favorite book, which is religious, or bringing a religious item for show and tell. The teacher should merely ensure that other students in the class understand that the book or other speech is expressing the student's religious belief and not the school's or the teacher's.

Unfortunately, it is Christian teachers and school officials who are sometimes the most reluctant to permit students to exercise their religious free speech rights in class. One child's Christian teacher refused to permit the child to read a Bible story in class when the teacher invited students to bring in their favorite book to share. Our attorneys learned that the teacher did not want to permit the expression of non-Christian religious viewpoints and, therefore, restricted the Christian viewpoints as well. Our attorneys discussed with the teacher the Christian belief that when the Gospel message is presented, God will not render the sharing of His Word void, even if there are competing religious or non-religious views also being expressed. The teacher should legally permit student religious expression.

May the Bible be taught as part of the academic curriculum?

The Supreme Court has held that public schools may teach students about the Bible as long as such teaching is presented in an objective manner as part of the school's secular academic program of education. The school curriculum may include objective study *about* religion as an important part of a complete education. Such an objective and academic education about the Bible is consistent with First Amendment principles and is broadly supported even by liberal legal organizations.

In the *Abington* case in 1963, when the Supreme Court prohibited only the *devotional* use of the Bible and other religious materials in the public school classroom. At the same time, the Court affirmed the continued *educational* use of religious material in public school. The key here is that the public school approach to religion must be academic, not devotional or proselytizing.

> *One court held that to not allow students to study about the Bible and religion "would give students a truncated view of our culture."*

In general, teachers must remember that as agents of the state they violate the Establishment Clause if they promote a devotional or proselytizing religious expression. However, a good teacher must also recognize what the Supreme Court recognized in the *McCollum* case, that "for good or ill, nearly everything in our culture worth transmitting, everything which gives meaning to life, is saturated with religious influences."

One federal appeals court held in the *Florey* case that to not allow students to study about the Bible and religion "would give students a truncated view of our culture." This court noted that while students and staff members must be excused from participating in practices contrary to their religious beliefs, there is no question that all courts approve the academic study of religion in a public school curriculum "when presented objectively as a part of a secular program of education."

The U.S. Department of Education has said that public schools "may not provide religious instruction, but they may teach about religion, including the Bible or other scripture." In keeping with the First Amendment's mandate of governmental neutrality toward religion, any study of religion in public school must be educational, not devotional or proselytizing. This principle holds true whether teaching about the Bible occurs in literature, history, or any other class, and whether the course is required or is an elective.

Where may the Bible be included in a public school's academic curriculum?

The Supreme Court has said that study about religion belongs in the public school curriculum wherever it naturally arises. A public school teacher may not promote a particular religion within the classroom (nor may a teacher denigrate religion).· However, a teacher may engage in teaching about the Bible wherever it falls naturally into the academic course outline.

> *Religion is very important in understanding the symbolism of Western literature.*

One place where the Bible clearly arises naturally in an academic context is in the English curriculum. Religion is very important in understanding the symbolism of Western literature. History is another subject area where religious issues naturally arise and can be dealt with from an academic perspective. Art and music likewise often portray religious themes, which students should understand from an academic and artistic perspective. Courses in the history of religion or in comparative religion are also appropriate for public schools.

In the case of *Stone v. Graham*, decided in 1980, when the Supreme Court banned posting of the Ten Commandments in public schools unless for some non-religious educational purpose, the Court was also careful to point out that "the Bible may constitutionally be used in an appropriate study of history, civilization, ethics, comparative religion or the like."

Another federal court noted in the case of *Wiley v. Franklin*, in 1979:

> The Bible is replete with writings relevant to such secular subjects and interests as history, both ancient and modern, literature, poetry, music, art, government, social customs and practices, values, behavioral sciences, and, more generally speaking, that broad range of subjects, values, interests, and activities encompassed within the generalized phrase "Western Civilization."

What constitutes objective, neutral, and academic classroom teaching about religion?

The constitutionality of teaching about religion in public schools depends upon such factors as how the class is taught, who teaches it, and what instructional materials and lessons are used. Any instruction about the Bible must be neutral, objective, and academic. Instruction about religion should neither promote nor disparage any religion, nor should either religion or the Bible be taught from any one particular sectarian point of view. All instruction should be neutral, objective and academic.

The constitutionality of public school instruction about the Bible is also affected by who teaches the class. A superintendent or school board should select teachers for a class about religion or the Bible in the same manner as all other teachers are selected—by their academic qualifications. Teachers should never be chosen or denied employment because of their or the school board's religious beliefs or training or lack thereof.

The educational materials used to instruct students about religion and the Bible are also important. Outside sources may provide funding for an elective course in religion as long as the funds are contributed with no strings attached.

Decisions concerning instructional materials, including which translation of the Bible will be used in class, should remain under the control of the school board. The Bible may be used as a primary text, although it probably should not be the only text used for an elective course about religion or the Bible. A Bible course that is objective, neutral, and academic should not resemble a Sunday school class. There should be no devotional component. Discussions about miracles and the historicity of Bible events and characters should include evidence from outside the text itself. Students should be encouraged to share their own beliefs about such matters in classroom discussions.

Parents of all faiths need to be assured that the goals of instruction about religion and the Bible in public school are academic and not devotional or proselytizing. Parents also need to be assured by appropriate school policies that academic teaching about the Bible is not intended to either undermine or reinforce the beliefs of those who accept the Bible as sacred Scripture or of those who do not. Teachers who instruct about religion and the Bible in public schools may not impose their own religious viewpoints on their students. Neither may they denigrate the beliefs of any students. Their job is merely to present information about the Bible and about religion. Students are left to form their own religious beliefs within their families and churches.

This doctrine of public school neutrality recognizes that the inculcation of particular sectarian religious beliefs is the responsibility of parents and religious communities, not the public school. Unlike public schools, parents and churches are not required to be neutral and objective about all faith expressions.

A consensus has emerged among many diverse religious and educational groups about the appropriate role for religion in the public school curriculum. Both liberal and conservative legal and educational groups who want to avoid any religious indoctrination in public schools agree on the following general principles regarding the appropriate role for religion in the public school curriculum.

- The school's approach to religion is *academic*, not *devotional.*
- The school may strive for student *awareness* of religions, but should not press for student *acceptance* of any religion.
- The school may sponsor *study* about religion, but may not sponsor the *practice* of religion.
- The school may *expose* students to a diversity of religious views, but may not *impose, discourage, or encourage* any particular view.
- The school may *educate* about all religions, but may not *promote or denigrate* any religion.
- The school may *inform* students about various beliefs, but should not seek to *conform* them to any particular belief.

When teaching about the Bible in a public school, teachers must understand the important distinction between advocacy, indoctrination, proselytizing, and the practice of religion, all of which are unconstitutional, versus teaching about religion in an objective, nonjudgmental, academic, neutral, balanced, and fair manner, which is constitutional. For instance, a Catholic teacher may not impose her beliefs about Christianity on a Baptist student, and a Baptist teacher may not impose her beliefs about Christianity on a Catholic student. Instruction must be neutral, and the religious views of all students in the class must be equally respected. The teacher may discuss instance, but may not imply that one belief is true while the other is not.

Finally, parents should keep these guidelines in mind if their students are being taught about religions other than Christianity in the classroom. Such instruction must also be objective, neutral, and academic. There have been numerous instances when parents have correctly objected to teaching about Islam that becomes devotional and proselytizing, rather than merely academic. A classroom presentation of Islam and other non-Christian faiths that becomes devotional or proselytizing also violates the Constitution.

May a public school teach an elective course in world religions?

Given the importance and influence of religion in current events today, every public school should include some study about religion, especially at the secondary level, as a way for students to learn about all major world religions and what their proponents believe. Because religion plays such a significant role in history and culture, study about religion is essential for students to be able to understand both our nation and the world.

School districts should consider offering both a Bible elective and an elective in world religions. Such courses give students an opportunity to learn about a variety of religions. It is important, however, for public schools to stress that such electives are designed to offer a good education, and not to prefer any one religious faith or group over others.

How should a public school select teachers for elective Bible courses?

Teaching about the Bible, either in literature and history courses or in Bible electives, requires considerable preparation. Many school districts and universities offer in-service workshops and summer institutes for teachers to learn how to teach about the Bible in an objective, neutral, and academic manner.

When selecting teachers to teach Bible electives, school districts should look for teachers who have some academic background in religion. Teachers who have not already received such academic preparation may elect to take in-service training in Bible instruction before teaching the courses. Teachers who are competent in the subject area should teach elective Bible courses, just as with other academic subjects. Colleges that train teachers may begin to add Bible course training along with training in algebra and history. Eventually, religious studies may become a certifiable field, requiring at least an undergraduate minor, with the same state certification requirements as are used for other academic subjects.

How does instruction in the Bible fit into elementary education?

The study of family, community, culture, and other universal themes in education may involve some discussion of religion. Presently, some schools include the study of world religions, such as Islam, as a cultural topic. In contrast, many of these same schools ignore Christianity and the many ways in which Christianity has affected American culture. In other cases, students are only taught the negative implications of Christianity while learning the positive aspects of other religions. In many schools, students study all religious holidays except Christian holidays.

Since such early exposure to study about religion builds a foundation that students will use later in life, it is very important that all religions be given fair and equal treatment and that Christianity is not treated as an outcast. It is an unconstitutional establishment of religion when all religions are not treated equally in objective, neutral, and academic course material.

Students whose parents make the request must be permitted to opt out of any religiously objectionable course material. The home and church are the major educators for children in the area of religion and the school must respect the religious choices made by parents.

How can the Bible be included in a literature course?

Use of the Bible as an objective and academic curriculum tool is one of the ways the Supreme Court has approved the Bible for use in public school classrooms. Children who do not know the stories and symbolism of the Bible are unable to understand much of the classic literature of Western Civilization.

An elective course in the Bible as literature would focus on the Bible as a literary text, including both the Bible as literature and the Bible in literature. A primary goal of such a course would be basic Biblical literacy, becoming informed about the language, major narratives, symbols, and characters of the Bible. The course might also explore the influence of the Bible in classic and contemporary poems, plays, and novels.

The Bible could also be included in other general English classes where the literature reflects Biblical imagery. For instance, in a 1968 speech given on the day before his assassination, Martin Luther King, Jr. said this:

> We've got some difficult days ahead. But it doesn't matter with me now. Because I've been to the mountaintop . . . And I've seen the Promised Land. I may not get there with you. But I want you to know tonight, that we, as a people, will get to the Promised Land.

In order to grasp the full significance of those famous words, a student must be familiar with the Biblical material to which these words refer, such as "mountaintop" and "Promised Land."

In fact, students who have no knowledge of the Bible, which includes too many of today's students, will never be able to understand the civil rights movement, the Mayflower Compact, America's founding documents, or President Ronald Reagan's "Shining City on a Hill" address. Students cannot read Milton's Paradise Lost, Camus' The Fall, Charles Dickens' A Tale of Two Cities, Ernest Hemingway's The Old Man and the Sea, or Leon Uris' Exodus without a basic understanding of the Bible.

Students cannot understand references in literature to Adam and Eve, Cain and Able, David and Goliath, or the Last Supper without understanding the Bible. Other words and phrases and literary allusions regularly used in Western literature have no context outside of a basic understanding of the Bible; including common literary phrases such as "being crucified," "cast your bread on the water," "a drop in the bucket," "mustard seed," "my cup runneth over," "a lamb to the slaughter," and "casting pearls before swine," to name only a few.

Literature classes offer a perfect opportunity for an academic study of Biblical words and concepts—including the Christian concepts of sacrificial death and salvation. In this context, even a discussion of salvation would be permissible in an objective and neutral academic environment, without any hint of proselytizing or establishment of a religion in violation of the First Amendment. In such a context, the teacher should never ask the students who is saved, or offer a salvation invitation. Such a discussion of salvation must be purely academic and set in the context of an understanding of Western literary concepts. Nevertheless, in learning to understand these concepts, the student also achieves an objective knowledge of how to be saved.

A book such as the Psalms would be an appropriate selection for student reading, when chosen for its literary and stylistic content.

> *Children who do not know the stories and symbolism of the Bible are unable to understand much of the classic literature of Western Civilization.*

When offering such religious material as part of the academic curriculum, the teacher should be careful to make clear to the students that use of this material is for educational purposes only and is not intended to either encourage or discourage them from a belief in the religious messages offered in the material. This sort of disclaimer should precede all classroom discussions about religious material.

The teacher must also be careful not to slip into a devotional or proselytizing discussion of religious material, but to keep the classroom discussions and questions neutral, objective, and academic in nature. Nevertheless, students can learn a great deal about the truths of Scripture in this manner from a good teacher.

When course work or an assignment includes a religious perspective, the teacher must permit students to opt out of the course or assignment on religious grounds without penalty. In such cases, the teacher must make an appropriate alternative assignment for the student who opts out. Just as a religious student might opt out of reading a Harry Potter novel, a non-religious student might opt out of reading the Psalms for much the same reasons.

Teachers are in control of the academic curriculum in their classroom, unless a higher education authority, such as the school board, has implemented a policy contrary to the teacher's lesson plans. For instance, if the school board determines that no Biblical material (such as the Book of Psalms) may be studied in a literature class, the teacher is bound by that policy. The same would be true if the school board banned the required reading of Harry Potter books.

How can the Bible be included in a history course?

Little of Western history, particularly the history of America, can be fully understood without reference to the Bible. The study of all history offers numerous opportunities for study about the Bible.

Students might learn about the origins of Judaism, for example, including the history of the Jewish people and how this history impacts current events. In studying the history of the ancient world, students might look at how the Bible sheds light on the history and beliefs of both Jews and Christians. A study of the Reformation might include a discussion about how Protestants and Catholics differ in their interpretation and use of the Bible. Why did Martin Luther differ from the Catholic church of his day? What did he mean by the term "justification by faith alone"? These are all appropriate academic discussions for the history classroom.

Throughout American history, the Bible has been the foundation for many public policy debates and social movements, such as the abolition of slavery, temperance, and the civil rights movement.

There are many opportunities for students studying U.S. history to learn about the role of religion and the Bible in American history and culture. For example, many historical documents, including many presidential addresses and congressional debates, contain Biblical references. Throughout American history, the Bible has been the foundation for many public policy debates and social movements, such as the abolition of slavery, temperance, and the civil rights movement. The history of the modern civil rights movement is similarly bathed in theology. No student can fully understand Martin Luther King Jr.'s "Letter From A Birmingham Jail" without studying the Christian theological context in which it was written.

A government or civics course should include some discussion of the Biblical sources for parts of our legal system. Students cannot understand the Mayflower Compact, America's founding documents (particularly the Declaration of Independence), George Washington's "Farewell Address," or President Ronald Reagan's more recent "Shining City on a Hill" speech without understanding the religious viewpoints of the Pilgrims, the Founding Fathers, and America's Presidents. A discussion of such religious topics is entirely appropriate in the context of a neutral, objective, and academic study of American (or world) history. For instance, the Bible was quoted more than any other source in America's founding documents.

> *A government or civics course should include some discussion of the Biblical sources for parts of our legal system.*

It is extremely important that public school teachers preserve the historic theological perspective of America's founders, particularly in light of the historical revisionism found in many modern American history textbooks. Inclusion of such religious material in a public school history class as part of a neutral, objective, and academic curriculum is not an unconstitutional establishment of religion. The idea behind such a curriculum is to inform students about American history, not to proselytize them.

May teaching about religious holidays be included in the public school curriculum?

Teaching about religious holidays may be included in the public school curriculum as long as the inclusion is strictly for an educational purpose and the instruction is given in an objective and neutral manner. Religious holidays in particular offer unique opportunities for objective religious instruction in both elementary and secondary schools. Such objective instruction is quite different from actually celebrating the religious holiday in the school program, which is not permissible.

Religious symbols may be used as teaching aids in studying various cultures and religions. The key in the public school classroom is for the teacher to broaden the education about religion. She may not limit teaching to one particular faith expression, such as studying Christmas but not Hanukkah or Ramadan.

Most public school officials have no problem with their students studying The Day of the Dead or the Chinese New Year, both of which have religious as well as cultural significance. In sharp contrast, many of those same schools prohibit any mention of Christmas. Yet, Christmas continues to be a national holiday and students should be taught about its origins in the same way they are taught about the origins of other national holidays and holidays celebrated by other religions. In today's America, fear of lawsuits, intimidation and outright deliberate misinformation about what is permitted in schools have created a public education system that too often fails to teach students about the American culture of which they are a part.

The key to teaching about holidays, as well as about other religious material in the school curriculum, is to make sure that the instruction is objective, neutral, and academic; that the study is not an actual celebration of the holiday, but is merely instruction about the holiday; and that students are permitted to opt out of the course or activity without penalty or comment if participation would violate their own religious beliefs.

> *Neutrality means that a school curriculum that studies Islam must also include instruction about Christian beliefs that also have cultural significance.*

The study of religious and national holidays, conducted in a neutral, objective, and academic manner is very instructive for public school children and helps them understand one another's culture. While this concept is generally understood regarding non-Christian cultures by today's schools, it is not always so clear when the instruction concerns the Christian culture. Neutrality means that a school curriculum that studies Islam must also include instruction about

Christian beliefs that also have cultural significance. Christianity may neither be the only religion excluded from or included in the classroom. Nor should Islam be taught as only "good" while Christianity is presented as only "bad."

What should a teacher do if specifically told by superiors not to teach a particular religious concept or holiday in the classroom?

Teachers do not have "free speech" or "free exercise" rights to teach religious concepts in their public school classrooms, even if they do so objectively, neutrally, and academically. While teachers generally have academic control of their classroom and curriculum, they are also under the direct control of their school superiors—the principal, superintendent, curriculum committees, and school board—in that order. If told by a superior that a particular religious concept or holiday may not be taught in the classroom, and if that instruction is not rescinded by a higher school authority, the teacher is mandated to follow the school's religious instruction policy. For instance, one teacher was terminated after he taught religious concepts of creationism in his class on evolution. When he argued that he had a free exercise right to teach the creation material, the court denied his defense and upheld his termination on the basis of insubordination.

Courts generally respect the right of school boards, and their delegated school administration and committees, to set overall public school curriculum policies, unless the policy violates the Establishment Clause. While teachers in today's classroom environment have the opportunity to instruct students about religion, they do not have a right to do so in violation of an established school curriculum policy. The problem in most schools today is that school officials incorrectly believe that even objective, neutral, and academic instruction about religion (particularly about Christianity) is an automatic violation of the Establishment Clause.

May a teacher include religious music in music classes or choral programs?

Religious music may be performed in public school choral programs or music classes if the religious music is included for a non-religious purpose and is only one part of a secular concert or program of education that includes a "full range of music, poetry and drama that is likely to be of interest to the students and their audience." As the *Florey* court explained, religious art and music have "developed an independent secular and artistic significance" in our culture, and to exclude them from public school classes and performances "would give students a truncated view of our culture." Singing religious music is not devotional when it is a subordinate part of a secular public school music class or concert setting, but has general historical and cultural value within its artistic context. Music teachers may include religious music as part of a secular program, but should be careful to choose a variety of music, both secular and sacred, and should choose music from various religious perspectives. One court upheld the choice of a religious song as a school choir theme song because the group had secular reasons for the choice. Legitimate secular reasons for choosing to perform religious music are: (1) that such music is generally respected artistically; (2) the composers are well respected; (3) such music is useful for teaching sight reading, and (4) such music is useful for learning a capella singing.

> *Public school music teachers should select sacred music pieces for their artistic or cultural, not their religious, value.*

The Supreme Court has said that "music without sacred music" would be "truncated and incomplete." For this same reason, a school could even have a Gospel Music Choir as one music group choice among many others. Choir members should be excused from participating in presentations in churches or religious settings that would offend their own religious beliefs.

From a legal perspective the questions for a court would be:

(1) What is the secular purpose of the religious music? and (2) Is there a mix of secular and sacred songs? A school-sponsored holiday (i.e., Christmas) concert containing only Christian music would be unconstitutional, but a program that included songs that mention God and other religious themes, along with secular songs, is perfectly appropriate in public school concert settings or music classes. Banning any song merely because it mentions God or a religious theme would limit the cultural perspective of a concert as well as the student's exposure to great music.

The selection of music for a concert, even a Christmas or holiday concert, has the secular purpose of teaching culture, not religion. Public school music teachers should select sacred music pieces for their artistic or cultural, not their religious, value. In the *Bauchman* case a public school was sued based partly on the fact that its choir performed religious music. In dismissing the *Bauchman* case, the court noted that "the Constitution does not require that the purpose of every government-sanctioned activity be unrelated to religion." The court also recognized that "a significant percentage of serious choral music is based on religious themes or texts. . . . Any choral curriculum designed to expose students to the full array of vocal music culture therefore can be expected to select a significant number of religious songs." Finally, the court held that "a vocal music instructor would be expected to select any particular piece of sacred choral music, like any particular piece of secular choral music, in part for its unique qualities useful to teach a variety of vocal music skills (i.e., sight reading, intonation, harmonization, expression)." As long as it is clear that a teacher has selected a piece of music for other than its religious significance, the choice will be upheld.

Just as with other curriculum areas in public school, the classroom teacher is not the ultimate determiner of music curriculum matters. If a teacher disobeys a direct order from a superior prohibiting the use of sacred music in class or concert settings, the teacher could be terminated for insubordination and a court would likely uphold the decision. Nevertheless, the Establishment Clause does not require a public school to ban all sacred music, and the school may not treat religion or religious music with hostility.

May a teacher display religious artwork on schoolroom walls?

For the same reasons that sacred music is permitted as part of a secular music or concert program, sacred art is also permitted as part of a secular program of art education. If students are given a choice of topics for artistic expression, a student may choose to produce artwork with a religious theme. Teachers may also teach art concepts using religious art demonstrating the concepts taught, as long as the artwork is part of a program of secular instruction. A teacher could not include only religious art; nor could she assign required religious artwork. But, when students are given a choice of expression, a religious choice may not be excluded.

The next question that arises is whether student religious artwork may be displayed along with secular artwork on schoolroom walls or in hallways. The answer is that the religious artwork may be displayed as long as the display does not give the impression of school endorsement of a particular religion. It is ironic that in today's American school, hallways are often decorated with voodoo masks or images of Aztec gods that students have made in art class. Witches and wizards line school walls at Halloween and classes read Harry Potter books, even though these images and concepts also represent the Wiccan faith. It seems that only Christian expression is challenged.

> *If students are given a choice of topics for artistic expression, a student may choose to produce artwork with a religious theme.*

Religious artwork, including Christian themes, may be displayed along with other secular artistic creations by students without violating the Establishment Clause. If requested to do so by school officials, the teacher may provide a disclaimer that the religious artwork does not represent the viewpoint of the school, but only of the student. Generally, however, the display itself provides evidence that the diverse artwork was created by the students and does not demonstrate official endorsement by the school of any one particular religious viewpoint.

No student may either be required to produce religious artwork or prohibited from creating religious artwork when a choice of subjects is offered. When the student makes a religious choice, his artistic religious creation may not then be subjected to what the Supreme Court calls "unique disabilities" merely because of the religious theme. A student's religious art would be subjected to a unique disability if the student were denied the opportunity to display his work merely because of its religious theme.

May teachers permit students to choose religious material to fulfill assignments or reading requirements?

If a teacher permits students to choose the subject of a writing assignment or reading material, students may choose a religious subject to complete the assignment. For example, a teacher might consider permitting students to select material to read during their free reading time or to use for writing book reports. The students may then choose to read religious material such as the Bible, religious magazines, or the Koran. Teachers must remember, however, that they would violate the Establishment Clause by promoting one particular religious choice or by encouraging students to read or complete assignments from the perspective of one particular religion.

> *Public school music teachers should select sacred music pieces for their artistic or cultural, not their religious, value.*

Choices may be offered in elementary, junior high, or high school assignments. For instance, when kindergarten students are permitted to choose material to share with their classmates in show-and-tell times, the children may choose to share religious material without violating the Establishment Clause. Teachers should always control their own classrooms and should understand and be sensitive to the various religious perspectives that are represented in the student population of a particular class. When a child chooses a religious topic or item, the teacher should always make sure other students understand that the religious viewpoint is the student's and that other students need not agree since each student's individual religious beliefs may differ.

In a high school class, a student might choose to give a persuasive speech about religion. Here again, the teacher may make a disclaimer regarding the religious content of the speech, but should not prohibit a religious choice if a choice of topic was offered. Permitting a religious choice does not violate the Establishment Clause ("separation of church and state") because student viewpoints or expressions are not capable of violating the Establishment Clause. Homework or class work with a religious theme should be judged by ordinary academic standards.

Must a school permit students to opt out of a religiously objectionable class or assignment?

Requests to opt out of religiously objectionable classes or assignments most often occur when Christian students are subjected to indoctrination in non-Christian religions. This was the case in a school district where teachers were requiring students to study Islam. Students were actually instructed on how to pray in the name of Allah, encouraged to role play as members of the Islamic faith, encouraged to engage in such Islamic devotional practices as reciting verses from the Koran and wearing clothing representative of the Islamic religion. While some courts reasoned that such instruction was merely cultural, schools should be required to treat all religions equally. To be neutral, this school should then have required Muslim children to role-play as Christians, memorize Christian Bible verses, and participate in Christian devotional activities. It is not likely a court would have viewed these equivalent Christian assignments as "cultural."

Students may not be required in school to speak in a manner that directly conflicts with their religious beliefs.

Students may not be required in school to speak in a manner that directly conflicts with their religious beliefs. Forcing a student to do so is, on the one hand a violation of the Establishment Clause and, on the other hand, a violation of the student's right not to speak, a corollary of the First Amendment right to freedom of speech.

Public schools and their officials may not impermissibly force objectionable speech by students or burden the religious beliefs of students, or violate parental rights. Before it may force a student to engage in religiously objectionable activities, a school must prove that it has a compelling reason for requiring a student to participate in a particular assignment and that this participation is the least restrictive means to accomplish the state's educational objectives. Otherwise, the school must accommodate the student's First Amendment right to the free exercise of religion and right not to speak by permitting the child to opt out of the objectionable religious activity or class.

The teacher may not go beyond mere impartation of knowledge about religion to the student, whether the information imparted is regarding Islam, Christianity, Judaism, or any other religion. Even when the activity does not go beyond mere impartation of knowledge, the school must permit a student who objects on religious grounds to opt out of the objectionable class or activity upon request of the parent.

According to the Supreme Court, there are two key fundamental interests served by public education. They are (1) inculcating "fundamental values" necessary for students to be citizens in a democratic system; and (2) equipping students with the basic skills necessary to be self-sufficient in modern society. A school may go no farther in requiring student participation in religiously objectionable courses or activities. Forcing the children of objecting parents to engage in instruction about religion in the classroom violates the parents' legally recognized right to direct their children's education and upbringing.

While opt out situations more often arise when Christian parents want to exclude their children from objectionable non-Christian instruction about religion, Christian teachers must be aware that the same right must be available for non-Christian parents when the instruction about religion involves Christianity and the Bible. In such cases, the teacher should work with the parent to provide comparable activities for the non-Christian child. The teacher must also be careful not to express a value judgment or to treat the child who is opting out any differently from the rest of the class.

May a voluntary reading program include religious books?

Voluntary reading programs may include a choice of religious books for students. Christian fiction suitable for children is widely available in today's publishing world, and such classic works should be included in the school library.

John Bunyan's Pilgrim's Progress, for example, was first published in 1678 and has been translated into more than seventy languages. Bunyan's vivid characters and unforgettable imagery have become part of our English vocabulary. The English language has been enriched by such colorful phrases from Bunyan as "vanity fair," "worldly-wise," "slough of despond," "city of destruction," "celestial city," and "house beautiful." Pilgrim's Progress was originally written for the masses, and critics now universally agree that it is one of the world's masterpieces.

General Lew Wallace's best-selling novel of the nineteenth century, Ben-Hur: A Tale of the Christ (1880), has sold millions of copies. Lloyd C. Douglas' The Robe (1942) is another classic with a religious theme. Bearing only a slight resemblance to the movie storyline of Ben-Hur, the novel traces what might have happened to Jesus' robe after the crucifixion and how the story of the crucifixion impacted people who came in contact with Jesus' discarded garment. Another popular classic that inspired the recent "What Would Jesus Do?" (WWJD) movement is Charles M. Sheldon's In His Steps.

Other popular books with a Christian worldview are J.R. Tolkien's Lord of the Rings, and C.S. Lewis' The Lion, the Witch and the Wardrobe and others in these two series for children. Lewis' Screwtape Letters would also be appropriate for older students.

Teachers should keep all of these books in mind along with

similar secular books for voluntary extracurricular reading. They are also appropriate substitutes for children whose parents disapprove of the Harry Potter book series, which promotes a Wiccan worldview. Children whose parents disapprove of reading from a Christian worldview should also be permitted to opt out and choose another appropriate assignment.

One popular year-round reading program, the Accelerated Reader Program (ARP), involves over 50,000 schools and provides schools with a list of over 100,000 pre-screened books that students may read to earn points. Students select their own reading material from the list, read at their own level and pace, and take computer-friendly multiple-choice tests to verify that they have read the book. If students pass the test, they earn points that may be spent on such prizes as pencils, books or certificates. All the classic literature mentioned above should be available in such reading programs.

Christian public school students involved in ARP complained about the offensive nature of books that offered higher point totals in the program and asked if they could earn the higher points by reading books of the Bible. The idea was approved by ARP and outside volunteers were asked to develop the fact check computer tests that would be used to validate the reading for the Bible.

All public school students are permitted to choose books of the Bible as part of their school's reading program. In fact, students at some schools have even purchased their own copies of the Bible so they do not need to wait for the return of a checked-out copy provided by a volunteer donor.

ARP officials approved all 66 books of the Bible for reading to earn points. Because such reading programs are voluntary and because students have free choice in the selection of books, attorneys have given the program an "all clear" legally for use in any school setting. When the Bible and other classic books from a Christian worldview are merely a few of many approved books in a secular reading program, they are a proper choice for such voluntary reading.

May religious books be included in the school library or in a teacher's classroom library?

It is both appropriate and legal to include Bibles and other religious books and material in the school library. One federal court ordered a school to put the Bible back on the library shelves, remarking that it was "inconceivable that the Bible should be excluded from a school library." Religious books from all religious faiths should be included in the school library. Without the availability of such books for students, their educational opportunities would be considerably curtailed.

The question of which books a teacher may keep in a classroom library is somewhat less clear. In one case, where it appeared that the teacher had been using religious books in the classroom to proselytize students, a court ruled that the religious books must be removed. However, where religion is part of the academic curriculum in the classroom, teachers should be permitted to keep reference books in the classroom library in the same manner as such classroom reference books would be appropriate for other academic subjects. The only exception would be where teachers have been specifically told not to keep religious books in the classroom library. In that situation, students would need to obtain the books from the school library.

May courses stressing values and morals be included in the school curriculum?

Public school teachers are permitted to teach values and character building in a non-religious manner in the classroom, even if the values and moral codes taught are identical to those taught by various religious groups. Teachers may promote values such as truth, compassion, sharing, and abstinence from destructive habits as positive secular values for society, but they may not look to religious moral codes such as the Ten Commandments as the sole authority for these values.

May teachers teach creation in biology classes that study evolution?

Teachers do not have a "free speech" or "free exercise" right to teach creationism in a public school classroom. Courts have consistently (although unreasonably, in our view) held that creationism, even "scientific creationism" is religion, while evolution is science. Therefore, the "religion" of creationism may only be presented in the same manner as any other objective religious belief in a public school classroom, and not as a scientific theory. Any teaching of creationism must follow the guidelines for other teaching about religion in public schools. Teachers must remember, with creationism as well as other religious instruction in public school, that the school board has the ultimate responsibility for determining the school curriculum, including what is taught to students in science class. Therefore, the teacher has a responsibility to abide by the school's policy in this regard. A school policy may permit teachers to choose to present views that oppose evolution.

> *When mentioning emerging theories such as "intelligent design," it is not necessary to define who the "designer" might be.*

As scientific study advances in the area of evolutionary theories, objective scientific evidence is emerging that actually disproves the theory of macroevolution. Teachers are permitted to teach this new scientific evidence disproving macroevolution, even while avoiding scientific claims that support creation. However, if the school board has mandated that teachers may not present scientific information that contradicts evolution, the teachers must follow such policies or risk termination.

The legality of presenting new theories of origins, such as intelligent design, in the public school classroom is not yet settled. Policies in these areas are set by state and local boards of education and teachers are required to follow whatever policies are set locally. If no policy prohibits it, teachers have academic freedom to design the curriculum and could include such scientific evidence disproving evolution as the scientific theory of "intelligent design," as well as a neutral, objective and academic presentation of the "religion" of creation. Some teachers approach this subject area by teaching about the controversy in society between the theories of creation and evolution.

Teachers who want to teach the concept of "intelligent design" (which does not make any conclusions about who or what the "designer" is) could include the theory as a subset of evolution if not otherwise prohibited from doing so. When mentioning emerging theories such as "intelligent design," it is not necessary to define who the "designer" might be. The teacher should let the students draw their own conclusions.

Students are always permitted to share their own religious viewpoints about evolution and creation in classroom discussions where the subject naturally arises.

School boards should not, however, mandate that teachers teach these emerging new scientific concepts such as "intelligent design" in science class. A better approach is to merely permit such teaching for those teachers who wish to do so. One case in which the teaching of "intelligent design" was held to be unconstitutional was a situation in which the teaching had been mandated by the school board, rather than permitted. It is probably also preferable for teachers to use the emerging scientific concepts from "intelligent design" to show the scientific problems associated with the theory of evolution rather than as a distinct theory in itself. Since evolution itself appears to have an irrational religious status with many in the scientific and philosophical communities (although courts have not yet recognized this fact), issues involving evolution take on incredible emotional baggage for their adherents.

Teachers may avoid endorsing a particular religion and "teach the controversy" by bringing in various outside speakers to discuss differing perspectives about origins or by permitting students to engage in classroom debates, if these topics are permitted in the school curriculum. If the teacher provides students with a free choice of special projects for a course in evolution, the teacher may permit students to make the choice to include a religious viewpoint in their project.

Students are always permitted to share their own religious viewpoints about evolution and creation in classroom discussions where the subject naturally arises. Only the teacher is capable of violating the Establishment Clause if the teacher discusses her own religious viewpoint about creation in the classroom. Students, as consumers of state instruction, and not paid agents of the state, are incapable of violating the Establishment Clause, even when they freely express their religious viewpoints in class or in special projects. Teachers can take advantage of this free speech right of students to allow the full truth about origins to be discussed in the classroom.

May a public school open the school day with a "moment of silence" that includes the opportunity for individual student prayer?

Since the 1960s, courts have held that it is unconstitutional to have an official prayer at the start of the school day. Students may not recite the Lord's Prayer in unison. Teachers may not ask for student volunteers to pray in front of the class.

More recently, officially sponsored prayer is also prohibited at events that form a part of the school's extracurricular program. For example, use of the public address system by students or clergy to deliver a prayer prior to sports events, such as football games, is no longer permitted. It does not matter that student volunteers conduct an official prayer, that attendance at such events is voluntary, or that no one is required to listen or participate. However, students who spontaneously gather for prayer before a sporting event, on their own, with no participation by school officials do not violate the Establishment Clause. Teachers are still not permitted to actively participate, however.

A new initiative has developed to return some solemnity to the start of the school day. Some states and school districts have initiated a "moment of silence" in which students may either pray silently or merely reflect on whatever thoughts they wish. These laws have been upheld where a court has determined that the state legislature or school board did not intend to favor any one particular religion or to favor religion over non-religion. A non-religious student may utilize a time of silent reflection in the same manner as a religious student. Every teacher knows it is impossible to discern what is going on in the mind of the student.

Since the 1960s, courts have held that it is unconstitutional to have an official prayer at the start of the school day.

The Supreme Court has said that a public school may provide a "moment of silence" at the start of the school day where the statute or policy authorizing the "moment of silence" has a clearly secular purpose. However, the Court has also said that if the main purpose behind a "moment of silence" is to endorse religion and to return silent prayer to the classroom, the practice is unconstitutional. Therefore, teachers should never invite students to "pray" before beginning a moment of silence. A moment of silence is only constitutional if it provides students with an opportunity to "meditate, pray, or engage in any other silent activity." Teachers may not encourage only prayer.

What religious expression is appropriate for public school graduation exercises?

In 1992, the Supreme Court ended a long-standing tradition of state-sponsored prayer at public school graduation ceremonies. The Court ruled that it was unconstitutional for clerics to offer officially sponsored invocations or benedictions at public school graduation ceremonies. Even though the Supreme Court addressed only the role of clerics who were being directed by school officials in offering state-sponsored prayers during graduation ceremonies, other lower courts have since expanded this prohibition.

Therefore, the determination of what religious expression is constitutional for graduation exercises is dependent upon what federal court jurisdiction controls the law for a particular school district. If the jurisdiction has not prohibited all prayer at graduation, the question is controlled by local school board policy.

Some courts that have considered this issue do permit student-initiated graduation prayer policies. However, others, including the Third Circuit Court of Appeals, which includes Pennsylvania, New Jersey, and Delaware, do not permit a senior class to determine whether to include a student moment of solemnization, which could be a prayer, in high school graduation ceremonies. It is still an open question, however, whether students who are selected to give valedictory or salutatory speeches are permitted to include a prayer. Therefore, such policies are left to the individual school district. Some courts, however, have determined that prayers or religious references even in graduation speeches could be considered proselytizing, particularly if they are too specific in discussing Christian theology. The United States Supreme Court has not yet ruled on these questions so they are controlled by circuit court decisions and local school board policy or practice.

Religious prayer and other religious activities are always permitted in public school baccalaureate services sponsored by the community rather than by the school.

A list of court cases controlling various jurisdictions in included in the Appendix to this section. The policy we would prefer is a policy permitted in the Eleventh Circuit, which includes Florida, Georgia, and Alabama. The court there approved a school policy that permits graduating students to determine whether they want to have a solemnizing moment at their graduation ceremony. If the vote is affirmative, a student may be chosen by the other students to deliver that message. The message is thus the free choice of the student, without any input by school officials. Students selected by their peers may then offer a prayer, a reading, or some other solemnizing statement not to exceed a particular time limit. In jurisdictions where student-initiated prayer has not been specifically banned by a court, we recommend graduation prayer policies like the one approved by the Eleventh Circuit that permits the students to make decisions regarding their own graduation ceremony.

Interestingly, although some courts have banned prayers that are proselytizing, the United States Supreme Court has said, in its decision in Santa Fe banning prayer at football games, that school officials may not make judgments about whether a prayer or reference is "sectarian" or "proselytizing." These matters have yet to be clearly decided.

Most school district policies regarding graduation prayers and religious references in student speeches are far more restrictive than they are legally required to be. This area of law is still very unsettled. Ultimately, the Supreme Court will make a determination of the issue. In the meantime, there is one clear legal principle that seems to be emerging on the subject of graduation prayer and student speeches: the most important constitutional distinction appears to be whether school officials have any input into a decision to pray or into the content of any student-initiated prayer or speech. It is important, until the U.S. Supreme Court decides the matter for the entire nation, to check the controlling legal principle in each individual jurisdiction.

Religious prayer and other religious activities are always permitted in public school baccalaureate services sponsored by the community rather than by the school. Baccalaureate services may be held at school facilities or in churches. School personnel are permitted to attend and may participate in the religious activities, but only in their personal capacities. These services will be discussed in more detail in the next section regarding Community Outreach activities in public schools.

Key Cases that Permit Teaching about Religion and the Bible in Public School

Abington v. Schempp, 374 U.S. 203 (1963).

This is the key case bearing on this issue. While the United States Supreme Court prohibited the devotional use of religious materials in the public school classroom, such as prayer and Bible reading at the start of the school day, the Justices affirmed the educational use of religious materials in public schools. The Court said:

> It may well be that one's education is not complete without a study of comparative religion or of the history of religion and its relation to the advancement of civilization. It certainly may be said that the Bible is worthy of study for its literary and historic qualities. Nothing we have said here indicates that such study of the Bible or of religion, when presented objectively as part of a secular program of education, may not be effected consistently with the First Amendment.

Wiley v. Franklin, 468 F. Supp. 133 (E.D. Tenn. 1979); *supp. op.*, 474 F. Supp. 525 (E.D. Tenn. 1979), *supp. op.*, 497 F. Supp. 390 (E.D. Tenn. 1980).

American culture has been profoundly influenced by the Bible and that influence may be presented academically in the classroom. This Tennessee federal district court noted:

> The Bible is replete with writings relevant to such secular subjects and interests as history, both ancient and modern, literature, poetry, music, art, government, social customs and practices, values, behavioral sciences, and, more generally speaking, that broad range of subjects, values, interests, and activities encompassed within the generalized phrase "Western Civilization." To ignore the role of the Bible in the vast area of secular subjects such as herein above referred to is to ignore a keystone in the building of an arch, at least insofar as Western history, values and culture are concerned.

Stone v. Graham, 449 U.S. 39 (1980).

The United States Supreme Court recognized the cultural value of teaching about religion and the Bible even while it banned posting the Ten Commandments in public schools without some non-religious educational purpose. The Court was careful to point out:

> [T]he Bible may constitutionally be used in an appropriate study of history, civilization, ethics, comparative religion or the like.

Altman v. Bedford Cent. School Dist.. 245 F.3d 49 (2nd Cir. 2001).

"While schools have a constitutional duty to make certain that subsidized teachers do not inculcate religion, the Establishment Clause does not prohibit schools from teaching about religion." This includes Christianity as well as religions other than Christianity.

McCullum v. Bd. of Educ., 333 U.S. 203 (1948).

In dealing with the issue of inclusion of sacred music in a public school concert setting, the key is whether there is an objective mix of secular and sacred music and what secular purpose the music fulfills. Justice Jackson's comment in a concurring decision in this case is still good law:

> Music without sacred music, architecture minus the Cathedral, or painting without the Scriptural themes, would be eccentric and incomplete, even from a secular view. . . . One can hardly respect a system of education that would leave a student wholly ignorant of the currents of religious thought that moved the world society for a part in which he is being prepared.

The United States Supreme Court also noted the following:

> The fact is that, for good or ill, nearly everything in our culture worth transmitting, everything which gives meaning to life, is saturated with religious influences.

Florey v. Sioux Falls Sch. Dist., 619 F.2d 1311 (8th Cir.), cert. denied, 449 U.S. 987 (1980).

The Eighth Circuit Court of Appeals upheld the religion policy of the Sioux Falls School District (contained in this Appendix), which permitted students and staff members to be excused from participating in practices contrary to their religious beliefs, but which upheld a school district policy permitting use of sacred music where the primary purpose was secular and cultural. The court held that the primary purpose of the policy permitting use of sacred music was as follows:

> [T]he advancement of the student's knowledge of society's cultural and religious heritage, as well as the provision of an opportunity for students to perform a full range of music,

> poetry and drama that is likely to be of interest to the students and their audience.

Since there is no question that all courts approve the objective study of religion in a public school curriculum "when presented objectively as a part of a secular program of education," the court held:

> [T]o allow students *only* to study and *not* to perform [religious music when] such works . . . have developed an independent secular and artistic significance would give students a truncated view of our culture.

Board of Educ. v. Mergens, 496 U.S. 226 (1990).

Justice O'Connor stated, "there is a crucial difference between *government* speech endorsing religion, which the Establishment Clause forbids, and *private* speech endorsing religion, which the Free Speech and Free Exercise Clauses protect." The key to the correct application of the law is neutrality.

> [The] message is one of neutrality rather than endorsement . . . . "The Establishment Clause does not license government to treat religion and those who teach or practice it, simply by virtue of their status as such, as subversive of American ideals and therefore subject to unique disabilities."

Sease v. Sch. Dist. of Philadelphia, 811 F. Supp. 183 (E.D. Pa. 1993).

The court prohibited a school secretary from leading a student Gospel choir that practiced on school grounds after school and that performed exclusively religious music at community events, including churches. However, it should be noted that in light of other case law, despite the circumstances of this decision, it is generally permissible for a school to have a Gospel choir as long as it is only one of many vocal groups in the music program and as long as choir members are permitted to opt out of performances in religious settings, such as churches.

Rosenberger v. Univ. of Vir., 515 U.S. 819 (1995).

The Supreme Court has said that the Establishment Clause is honored when the state exhibits neutrality between various religions and between religion and non-religion. The Court held that a public university could not deny student funds to a religious student group that published a newspaper with an evangelical Christian perspective. Such equal support did not violate the Establishment Clause.

Doe v. Duncanville Indep. Sch. Dist., 70 F.3d 402 (5th Cir. 1995).

A school choir may have a religious theme song if there is a legitimate secular reason for the choice.

> Indeed, to forbid [the school district] from having a theme song that is religious would force [the district] to disqualify the majority of appropriate choral music simply because it is religious. Within the world of choral music, such a restriction would require hostility, not neutrality, toward religion. . . . A position of neutrality towards religion must allow choir directors to recognize the fact that most choral music is religious. Limiting the number of times a religious piece of music can be sung is tantamount to censorship and does not send students a message of neutrality.

Bauchman v. West High School, 132 F.3d 542 (10th Cir. 1997).

In this case the court dismissed a lawsuit brought by a student because, among other things, the school choir performed religious music. The court noted "the Constitution does not require that the purpose of every government-sanctioned activity be unrelated to religion."

The court also rejected the student's challenge to choir performances at religious sites such as churches. The court determined that a choir director could use religious sites for secular reasons, such as that they might be "acoustically superior to high school auditoriums" and would provide a "showcase [for] his choir to the general public in an atmosphere conducive to the performance of serious choral music." The court noted that the choir performed a number of different pieces, both religious and secular "all of which reflect the community's culture and heritage."

The court recognized that:

> [A] significant percentage of serious choral music is based on religious themes or text. Any choral curriculum designed to expose students to the full array of vocal music culture therefore can be expected to select a significant number of religious songs. Moreover, a vocal music instructor would be expected to select any particular piece of sacred choral music, like any particular piece of secular choral music, in part for its unique qualities useful to teach a variety of vocal music skills (i.e., sight reading, intonation, harmonization, expression).

Vaughn v. Reed, 313 F. Supp. 431 (W.D.Va.1970).

The court held that the Bible could be taught in a public school under the following guidelines:

1. Supervision and control of the course should be under the direction of the school board;
2. The school board should do the hiring and firing of teachers for the Bible course in the same manner as it does for all other courses;
3. Teachers should be state certified in the same manner as for all other academic subjects;
4. No inquiry should be made to determine the religious beliefs, or the lack thereof, of teacher applicants;
5. The school board should prescribe the curriculum and select all teaching materials, including the appropriate translation of the Bible;
6. The course should be offered as an elective and children who choose not to take the course should be offered a reasonable alternative course;
7. The school board may solicit contributions from private organizations to fund the costs of a Bible course, but such contributions shall be received with "no strings attached" other than the understanding that the funds are earmarked for the Bible course exclusively; and
8. The course should be taught in an objective manner with no attempt made to indoctrinate the children as to either the truth or falsity of the Biblical materials.

Hall v. Bd. of Conecuh County, 656 F. 2d 999 (5th Cir. 1981).

The issue in this case was whether the Bible Literature course was sufficiently secular in nature to survive constitutional scrutiny. The court disapproved the course, while affirming that, if taught for a secular purpose and in a neutral manner, such a class would be constitutional. The court found in this instance that the course "consisted entirely of a Christian religious perspective and within that a fundamentalist and/or evangelical doctrine." The court held that the textbook being used revealed a fundamentalist Christian approach to the study of the Bible and was devoid of any discussion of its literary qualities. Although the teacher was state certified, he was also a Baptist minister, which would not have disqualified him if the course had been taught in an objective and neutral manner. The court did not find that, in practice, the course lived up to the school board's statement of a secular purpose for the course. The examinations given in the course consisted primarily of rote memorization of the Bible, which was not consistent with the course methodology outlined in the course guide.

Crockett v. Sorenson, 568 F. Supp. 1422 (W.D. Va. 1983).

Although the court observed an actual class session and found that the lessons were presented in an objective manner and that the teaching methods were appropriate for the grade level (4th and 5th grades), and although the court found no attempt to indoctrinate the students in the tenets of any religious faith, the court nevertheless held that this particular Bible course was unconstitutional because it had been instituted as a religious exercise designed to inculcate religious beliefs in the students some 40 years earlier and had continued uninterrupted since then.

Despite holding that this particular Bible course was unconstitutional, the Crockett court outlined some important reasons why school children should be taught about the Bible. The court's discussion is so remarkable in its understanding of Biblical influences on our culture that it will be quoted in full here:

> In art, one cannot truly appreciate such great works as da Vinci's *Last Supper*, Michelangelo's work in the Sistine Chapel, or Albrecht Durer's woodcuts without some basic under-

standing of what the Bible contains. Without some introduction to the Book of Isaiah, Handel's *Messiah* loses much of its force and importance. Literature is replete with Biblical allusion. Some of the better known works which rely heavily on allusions from the Bible include Milton's *Paradise Lost*; the plays of Shakespeare, especially *Measure for Measure*; Blake's *Marriage of Heaven and Hell*; Melville's *Moby Dick*; Faulkner's *Absalom, Absalom*; T.S. Eliot's *The Wasteland*, and C.S. Lewis's *The Screwtape Letters*. Our language and popular culture are also replete with Biblical allusions. The symbol of the American Medical Association, a staff with a serpent on it, is drawn from an episode in the Book of Numbers, when Moses, at God's suggestion, raised a bronze serpent on a staff and all the children of Israel who looked upon it were healed of snakebites. The phrase "handwriting on the wall" comes from a passage in the Book of Daniel in which handwriting on the wall foretold rough times ahead for Babylonian King Belshazzar. The popular phrase "apple of my eye" is used in the Old Testament as one of God's descriptions for His people Israel. And, of course, the term "Armageddon" is the site where the battle will take place which will mark the end of the age, as described in the Book of Revelations. Anglo-American law as we know it today is also heavily indebted to principles and concepts found in the Bible. William Blackstone, one of the most influential figures in the development of the common law, explained, "The doctrine thus delivered we call the revealed or divine law, and they are to be found only in the holy scriptures…. Upon these two foundations, the law of nature and the law of revelation, depend all human laws. That is to say, no human laws should be suffered to contradict these." …Further, Biblical influences pervade many specific areas of the law. The "good Samaritan" laws use a phrase lifted directly out of one of Jesus' parables. The concept of the "fertile octogenarian," applicable to the law of wills and trusts, is in large part derived from the Book of Genesis where we are told that Sarah, the wife of patriarch Abraham,

> gave birth to Isaac when she was "past age." In addition, the Ten Commandments had an immeasurable effect on Anglo-American legal development. Moreover, we, as Americans, should especially be aware of the influence that the Bible and its principles have had on the founding and development of our nation. In this regard, it is significant that President Ronald Reagan, on February 3, 1983, issued a proclamation declaring 1983 the "Year of the Bible" in recognition of the Bible's fundamental and enduring influence on our country.

Gibson v. Lee County Sch. Bd, 1 F. Supp.2d 1426 (M.D. Fla. 1998).

While a court is required to be deferential to a state's articulation of a secular purpose, the court in this case issued an injunction against the teaching of a Bible as history course because it found that the course did not meet its stated secular purpose requirement of teaching history and not religion.

The court said: "The ultimate test of the constitutionality of any course of instruction founded upon the Bible must depend upon classroom performance. It is that which is taught in the classroom that renders a course" either constitutionally permissible or impermissible.

The court further held the following:

> If that which is taught seeks either to disparage or to encourage a commitment to a set of religious beliefs, it is constitutionally impermissible in a public school setting. If that which is taught avoids such religious instruction and is confined to objective and non-devotional instruction in Biblical literature, Biblical history and Biblical social customs, all with the purpose of helping students gain 'a greater appreciation of the Bible as a great work of literature' and source of 'countless works of literature, art and music' or of assisting students acquire 'greater insight into the many historical events recorded in the Bible' or of affording students greater insight into the 'many social customs upon which the Bible has had a significant influence" . . . . no constitutional barrier

would arise to such classroom instruction.

The court also said that a public school course may not "promote religion or Christianity in the guise of teaching history."

Holloman ex rel. Holloman v. Harland, 370 F.3d 1252 (11th Cir. 2004).

A teacher may not pray in class, but he or she may "study[] the Bible as part of a course on literature, or sing[] a religious hymn in a music class, or analyz[e] a prayer as a poem."

Miller v. Cooper, 244 P.2d 520 (N.M. 1952).

A court ruled that a teacher may not keep religious literature in the classroom, even if the teacher does not intend to distribute it to the students or to instruct the students to read it. Only curriculum-related literature should be kept in the classroom or distributed to students.

Engel v. Vitale, 370 U.S. 421 (1962).

The Court held that officially composed school prayers recited at the beginning of each school day violated the Establishment Clause of the First Amendment. The Abington case then also prohibited recitation of the Lord's Prayer.

Malnak v. Yogi, 592 F.2d 197 (3d Cir. 1979).

The court held unconstitutional a school course in which students participated in transcendental meditation ceremonies.

Hazelwood v. Kuhlmeier, 484 U.S. 260 (1988).

The Court permitted school officials to restrict student articles in the school newspaper, determining that the school newspaper was part of the school curriculum and could be restricted by school officials as long as they had a legitimate pedagogical reason for the restrictions.

Doe v. Duncanville Indep. Sch. Dist., 70 F.3d 402 (5th Cir. 1995).

A school employee may not pray with students and a coach may not pray with his team, even if the prayers are student-initiated. The teacher may, however, exercise deference or respect during student-initiated prayers.

Marchi v. BOCES, 173 F.3d 469 (2d Cir. 1999).

School officials may direct teachers not to include religious references in letters written to parents in their capacity as teachers. The letters are considered to be part of the school's instructional program, which is under the ultimate direction of school officials and the school board. The court did not answer the question of what freedom the teacher would have when not directed by superiors to refrain from this practice.

Doe v. Porter, 370 F.3d 558 (6th Cir. 2004).

A school allowed students from a local Bible college to come in and teach half-hour Bible classes to elementary students in a conservative, rural community. The Bible college students designed and taught the lessons without the school's review. The court found that the classes were overtly sectarian and advanced religion, and ordered the school to stop the classes and to pay the plaintiff's costs and attorney's fees.

Citizens for a Responsible Curriculum v. Montgomery County Public Schools, 2005 WL 1075634 (D.Md. 2005).

A school adopted into its health curriculum a "Myth/Fact" format course on homosexuality that contained such "myths" as "Homosexuality is a sin" and went on to explain that most religious leaders accepted an interpretation of the Bible that accepts homosexuality (except historically intolerant groups like Fundamentalists and Baptists, who hold a misguided interpretation of the Bible). The court expressed shock at "the willingness of Defendants to venture-or perhaps more correctly bound-into the crossroads of controversy where religion, morality, and homosexuality converge," and stated that "[t]he wisdom of approving a curriculum which prohibits students from discussing one viewpoint of a controversial subject goes to the very essence of that First Amendment faith." The school was ordered to stop using this course, which denigrated one particular Biblical view of homosexuality.

Pierce v. Society of Sisters, 268 U.S. 510 (1925).

The Court recognized the right of parents to direct the upbringing and education of their children in making decisions about education.

West Virginia Bd. of Educ. v. Barnette, 319 U.S. 624 (1943).

Public school opt out policies are based on the right to refrain from speaking, which is an implicit component of the First Amendment Right to Freedom of Speech. By permitting students to opt out of religiously offensive classes or activities, a public school recognizes that the government may not compel a person to speak about, endorse, or subsidize activities that are religiously objectionable to that person. This case permitted Jehovah's Witness students to opt out of the opening salute to the American flag. The Court emphasized:

> If there is any fixed star in our constitutional constellation, it is that no official, high or petty, can prescribe what shall be orthodox in politics, nationalism, religion, or other matters of opinion or force citizens to confess by word or act their faith therein.

Wisconsin v. Yoder, 406 U.S. 205 (1972).

The Court held that when parents' decisions about the education of their children are based on a free exercise right combined with the parental right to direct the religious upbringing of their children, the state's action that conflicts with parental decisions must be subjected to strict scrutiny. The United States Supreme Court recognized that parents have a "fundamental interest" in guiding "the religious future and education of their children." Indeed, "[t]his primary role of the parents in the upbringing of their children is now established beyond debate as an enduring American tradition." Therefore, a public school must respect the request of a parent to opt out his child from religiously offensive public school classes or activities.

Board of Educ. v. Pico, 457 U.S. 853 (1982).

The Court held there are two key interests served by public education. They are (1) inculcating the "fundamental values" that are necessary for students to be citizens in a democratic system and (2) equipping students with the basic skills necessary to be self-sufficient in modern society. School curricula are therefore to be geared to those two requirements and cannot go any further if doing so would infringe on a fundamental right, such as the right of parents to direct the education of their children. Therefore, unless a school's program serves a compelling state interest, the student must be accommodated in a request to opt out of a religiously offensive class or activity.

Herdahl v. Pontotoc County School Dist., 933 F.Supp. 582 (N.D.Miss. 1996).

A school offered elective Bible classes to elementary students during a curriculum rotation. The court held that the "elective" nature of the class did not provide a true opt-out policy because "young children are faced once a week with the difficult choice of conforming to the overwhelming majority's participation in the class or absenting themselves in protest." The court also noted that there was no genuine choice to decline the Bible classes because the alternative was to repeat another class in the rotation.

Southworth v. Grebe, 151 F.3d 717 (1998).

The court said:

> "The Supreme Court has long recognized two necessary corollaries to the First Amendment's guarantee of free speech: the right not to speak, and the right not to be compelled to subsidize others' speech."

Troxel v. Granville, 530 U.S. 57 (2000).

The Supreme Court reaffirmed the liberty interest of parents to care for and control their children's upbringing. The Court held that "[i]t is cardinal with us that the custody, care, and nurture of the child reside first in the parents, whose primary function and freedom include preparation for obligations the state can neither supply nor hinder."

Leebaert v. Harrington, 332 F.3d 134 (2nd Cir. 2003).

A parent objected to an entire health class curriculum and removed his son from the class. The school allowed students to opt out of the six days of the class during which AIDS and sex education were taught, but the teacher failed the student when he missed the entire class. The court backed the school, saying the parent did not have a fundamental right to except his child from the public school course requirements.

Blau v. Fort Thomas Public School Dist., 401 F.3d 381 (6th Cir. 2005)

The court rejected a school dress code challenge, stating:

> "The critical point is this: While parents may have a fundamental right to decide whether to send their child to a public school, they do not have a fundamental right generally to direct how a public school teaches their child. Whether it is the school curriculum, the hours of the school day, school discipline, the timing and content of examinations, the individuals hired to teach at the school, the extracurricular activities offered at the school or, as here, a dress code, these issues of public education are generally 'committed to the control of state and local authorities.'"

Cases Involving Issues of Creation/Evolution

Edwards v. Aguillar, 482 U.S. 578 (1987).

The United States Supreme Court has never mandated that Darwinism be taught as fact rather than theory; nor have judges ever prohibited teachers from teaching scientific evidence disproving evolution to public school students. In fact, while the Supreme Court said in this case that creation was a religion, the Court at the same time indicated its approval of a science curriculum that would teach much more than evolution. The Court said:

> Teaching a variety of scientific theories about the origins of humankind to schoolchildren might be validly done with the clear secular intent of enhancing the effectiveness of science instruction.

Webster v. New Lenox Sch. Dist., 917 F.2d 1004 (7th Cir. 1990).

A middle school teacher could not ignore instructions from superiors to cease teaching creation science in a social studies class. No teacher has a First Amendment right to teach material contrary to the orders of superiors.

Peloza v. Capistrano Sch. Dist., 37 F.3d 517 (9th Cir. 1994).

A high school biology teacher did not have a right to refuse to teach evolution in the classroom. The teacher had claimed that the school was requiring him to teach a religion in violation of the Establishment Clause. The court rejected the teacher's claim that evolution was a religion.

LeVake v. Independent School Dist. No. 656, 625 N.W.2d 502 (Minn. App. 2001).

When a high school teacher refused to teach evolution in his biology class without also teaching criticism of evolution, the school was justified in reassigning him to another class. The outcome of this case contradicts the decision of the U.S. Supreme Court in the

Aquillar case above.

No Child Left Behind Act of 2001, Pub. L. No. 107-110, 115 Stat. 852 (2002).

Congress endorsed teaching evolution in a more balanced manner. The Conference Committee report that accompanied President Bush's education initiative, noted:

> Where topics are taught that may generate controversy (such as biological evolution), the curriculum should help students to understand the full range of scientific views that exist, why such topics may generate controversy, and how scientific discoveries can profoundly affect society.

Kitzmiller v. Dover Area School Dist., 400 F.Supp.2d 707 (M.D.Pa. 2005).

A Pennsylvania judge ruled that requiring science teachers to read a statement identifying evolutionary origins as a theory and not proven fact and directing interested students to a book about Intelligent Design was a state endorsement of religion. In an unusually hostile decision, the judge claimed Intelligent Design was just an attempt by Christians to teach religion in public schools and was not science.

Reed v. Van Hoven, 237 F. Supp. 48 (W.D. Mich. 1965).

An earlier case had permitted a school to set aside "a few moments of silence . . . for private meditation" at the start of the lunch period, and the court held that this did not violate student's Free Exercise rights.

Gaines v. Anderson, 421 F. Supp. 337 (D.C. Mass. 1976).

A Massachusetts statute requiring the observance of a period of silence, not exceeding one minute, at the commencement of the first class of each day in all grades in all public schools for meditation or prayer was held to be constitutional because the court found that it had a secular purpose.

Wallace v. Jaffree, 472 U.S. 38 (1985).

The Alabama statutes considered by the Court authorized a one-minute period of silence for voluntary prayer or for teacher-led prayer, which the Court held to be unconstitutional because the Court found that the statute had no secular purpose and the sole purpose behind its enactment was to endorse religion. The Alabama legislation had escalated over several years from a minute of silence "for meditation," then for "meditation and voluntary prayer," and finally in 1982, for a state-prescribed prayer. The Supreme Court did not consider the original 1978 legislation authorizing a one minute period of silence "for meditation," which would likely have been upheld.

Justice O'Connor stated:

> A state-sponsored moment of silence in the public schools is different from state-sponsored vocal prayer or Bible reading. First, a moment of silence is not inherently religious. Silence, unlike prayer or Bible reading, need not be associated with a religious exercise. Second, a pupil who participates in a moment of silence need not compromise his or her beliefs.

During a moment of silence, a student who objects to prayer is left to his or her own thoughts, and is not compelled to listen to the prayers or thoughts of others. For these simple reasons, a moment of silence statute does not stand or fall under the Establishment Clause according to how the Court regards vocal prayer or Bible reading. "[T]he observance of a moment of reverent silence at the opening of class" may serve "the solely secular purposes of the devotional activities without jeopardizing either the religious liberties of any members of the community or the proper degree of separation between the spheres of religion and government."

Herdahl v. Pontotoc County School District, 933 F. Supp. 582 (N.D. Miss. 1996).

The court found that prayers delivered by volunteer students over the school intercom at the start of the school day were unconstitutional because the students hearing the prayers were a captive audience and the school intercom had not previously been opened as a public forum for student free speech. The school had argued that it was merely permitting a student group to engage in freedom of expression over the intercom.

Later, the students relied upon language the court had used, in passing, suggesting that students, including younger students with parental consent, could voluntarily meet for student-initiated, student-led prayer at school before the school day began. They began to hold before-school voluntary student prayer meetings, which at one time included 95% of the student body.

Brown v. Gwinnett County School District, 112 F.3d 1464 (11th Cir. 1997).

The court held that Georgia's Moment of Quiet Reflection in Schools Act did not violate the First Amendment. The Act authorized a brief period of quiet reflection "conducted by the classroom teacher in charge at the opening of school upon every school day for not more than 60 seconds with the participation of all the pupils therein assembled." The court found that the Act had a secular purpose because it was intended to simply provide students with an opportunity for a period of quiet reflection in the midst of a hectic world. The primary effect was not to advance or promote religion because the daily announcements for a "moment of silence" in no way suggested that students should or should not pray during this time.

This case came before the court when a teacher was fired for refusing to conduct the "moment of quiet reflection" in his classroom as the law required, alleging that the policy violated the Establishment Clause. The court disagreed.

Brown v. Gilmore, 258 F.3d 265 (4th Cir. 2001); *injunction petition denied*, 122 S.Ct. 1 (2001), *cert. denied*, 122 S. Ct. 465 (2001).

The Fourth Circuit Court of Appeals determined that a Virginia moment of silence law was constitutional. Chief Justice Rehnquist held that a public school could provide a "moment of silence" at the beginning of each school day because the authorizing statute had a clearly secular purpose.

Two main factors used in determining the constitutionality of the "moment of silence" were (1) whether the statute had a secular purpose, and (2) whether the minute of silence was being used as a time of collective prayer. The secular purpose involved providing a moment of quiet reflection in light of all the high-profile situations of violence taking place in public schools. The minute of silence was not being used to coerce students to pray or to lead them in a collective time of prayer. There was no evidence that the practice was being used as a state-sponsored prayer exercise.

Holloman ex rel. Holloman v. Harland, 370 F.3d 1252 (11th Cir. 2004).

A teacher could not ask for prayer requests and then observe a "moment of silence" before her math class every day.

Cases Involving Graduation Prayer

Stein v. Plainwell Comm. Schs., 822 F.2d 1406 (6th Cir. 1987).

The court held that ceremonial graduation invocations and benedictions which were given by students chosen from a group of honor students, where the individual students determined the content, did not violate the Establishment Clause.

Lee v. Weisman, 505 U.S. 577 (1992).

The United States Supreme Court held that clerics may not offer invocations or benediction prayers at graduation ceremonies in public schools. The prayers constituted official speech by the government since school officials made the decision that prayers should be given at the ceremony and the principal selected the person to give the prayer and directed the religious content of the prayer. These were official actions attributable to the government in violation of the Establishment Clause.

The two factors used in determining the constitutionality of such prayers were (1) whether the school, acting as the state, was endorsing religion and (2) whether students were compelled to participate. The court determined that the prayers were a state endorsement of religion, and students were compelled to participate because of peer pressure and a desire to participate in their graduation exercises. The case involved middle school students, who the court considered were of an impressionable age.

Jones v. Clear Creek Ind. Sch. Dist., 977 F.2d 964 (5th Cir. 1992).

An earlier decision by the Fifth Circuit had approved a school policy permitting students to decide by a majority vote whether to have prayer at graduation and who would deliver a nonsectarian prayer. In this case the court reexamined that ruling in light of *Lee v. Weisman* and held that the prayers would still be constitutional because they were at the discretion of students, given by students, and limited to being nonsectarian and non-proselytizing. Further, this case involved high school students, not the more impressionable middle school students in *Lee*. With regard to graduation prayers, each federal circuit court has developed its own post-*Lee* interpretation of what prayers are legally permissible.

Goluba v. Sch. Dist. of Ripon, 45 F. 3d 1035 (7th Cir. 1995).

The court held that a school could not be held in contempt of a court-ordered prohibition of school-sponsored prayer when several students spontaneously recited the Lord's Prayer at the graduation ceremony because the school had no advance knowledge. In a later case, the Sixth Circuit determined that permitting a nonsectarian invocation and benediction at a university graduation ceremony was constitutional.

ACLU of New Jersey v. Black Horse Pike Regional Board of Education, 84 F.3d 1471 (3rd Cir. 1996).

This court held that a school board policy allowing the senior class to vote to determine whether or not they wanted a moment of silence or prayer conducted by a student at graduation ceremonies violated the Establishment Clause because there was enough district control present in the policy to find a state endorsement of prayer. The court was also concerned that the vote permitted a plurality of students to impose their will on a minority group of classmates, who might then be required to decide between missing their graduation or participating in a prayer exercise to which they did not subscribe.

Committee for Voluntary Prayer v. Wimberly, 704 A.2d 1199 (D.C. Cir. 1997).

A proposed initiative to permit a student initiated, nonsectarian, nonproselytizing voluntary prayer, invocation, and/or benediction in public school during compulsory or noncompulsory school-related student assemblies, sporting events, graduation or commencement ceremonies, and other events was ruled unconstitutional. The initiative was found to have an impermissible purpose of fostering prayer in the public schools with the principal and primary effect of advancing the religious views of those students who led the prayers. Moreover, the initiative would place public school teachers and principals in the position of endorsing legislation that had the purpose of fostering prayer by students in public schools. The fact that some of the school-related events covered by the initiative were compulsory underscored the coercion which might be brought to bear on students who did not share the religious views of those students who initiated the prayer. The court found that subtle coercion existed even for noncompulsory school-related functions.

Chandler v. Siegelman, 230 F.3d 1313 (11th Cir. 2000).

The court clarified that "*Santa Fe* condemns school sponsorship of student prayer. *Chandler* condemns school censorship of student prayer." The court struck down a school policy that prohibited all prayer in the context of school events, stating that it was overbroad because it assumed that all speech at school events was school-sponsored. The court also held that a policy could not impose time, place, or manner restrictions on religious speech that it did not place on other kinds of speech.

Adler v. Duval County School Board, 250 F.3d 1330 (11th Cir. 2001).

The court held that the school district's policy of allowing the graduating class to decide whether to have a student of their choosing deliver a solemnizing message at graduation without monitoring or review by the school board was constitutional. The school board maintained no control over the decision of the students to have a message or over the contents of the message itself, which was at the discretion of the student selected. The policy had the secular purpose of promoting free speech by students and it did not advance religion or promote prayer since the selected student could pray or recite another solemnizing message of his choice. This policy is contained in this Appendix and is recommended for use by other schools in jurisdictions where courts have not specifically banned the practice.

Deveney v. Board of Educ. of County of Kanawha, 231 F.Supp.2d 483 (S.D.W.Va. 2002).

The court disapproved a school policy that allowed the senior class to vote on whether they wanted an invocation, and then to select a volunteer who would submit a non-sectarian, non-proselytizing, written invocation to school authorities for review (similar to the *Clear Creek* policy). The court held that the very term "invocation" (instead of "invocation or message) implied invoking divine attention, and that the review by school officials implied school control, making the prayer no longer private speech. These unconstitutional aspects are not present in the *Adler* policy.

Doe ex rel. Doe v. School Dist. of City of Norfolk, 340 F.3d 605 (8th Cir. 2003).

A school determined that it could not include an invocation in its graduation ceremony. At the beginning of the ceremony, the principal explained the decision not to include the prayer. During the ceremony, as was customary, a school board member was invited to make a speech, the content for which he was completely responsible. He chose to recite the "Lord's Prayer" without prior knowledge or approval of school officials. The court ruled that, because it was clear to attendees that the school board member spoke as a private citizen and not as a representative of the school, and because the school did not anticipate and could not control the content of the speech, the school could not be held responsible for what otherwise would have been a violation of the Establishment Clause.

Collins v. Chandler Unified Sch. Dist., 644 F.2d 759 (9th Cir. 1981).

An Arizona high school principal who permitted the student council to plan and schedule periodic student assemblies with voluntary attendance during the school day, violated the Establishment Clause when he also permitted the student council to recite prayers and Bible verses of their choosing. The permission for students to conduct prayers could not be saved from constitutional attack merely because attendance at school assemblies was voluntary.

Committee for Voluntary Prayer v. Wimberly, 704 A.2d 1199 (D.C. Cir. 1997).

A proposed initiative to permit nonsectarian, non-proselytizing student-initiated voluntary prayer at all student events, including invocations and/or benedictions at graduation or commencement ceremonies, was ruled unconstitutional because it had an impermissible purpose of fostering prayer in the public schools and it had a primary effect of advancing the religious views of those students who led the school prayers. The court found that subtle coercion existed even for noncompulsory school-related functions.

Coles v. Cleveland Bd. of Educ., 171 F.3d 369 (6th Cir. 1999).

The court ruled that the school board's practice of opening its meetings with prayer or a moment of silent prayer violated the Establishment Clause. The court held that the invocations had a coercive effect on students who had an incentive to attend the meetings to appeal suspensions or expulsions or for other matters. The prayers were deemed to be coercive because of the authority that the school board had over the students. The court ruled that since the meetings took place on school property, they were intertwined with the public school system and were to be treated like school prayers, which are prohibited under *Lee v. Weisman*, 503 U.S. 577 (1992), rather than like legislative prayers which are permissible under *Marsh v. Chambers*, 463 U.S. 783 (1983). In this case, the prayers were frequently sectarian and were regularly delivered by the school board president himself.

School boards located outside the Sixth Circuit (which includes Ohio, Kentucky, and Tennessee), may continue to have opening prayers as permitted for legislatures under the U. S. Supreme Court's decision in *Marsh v. Chambers*, which allows prayer in legislative bodies as a traditional practice. Since courts have also approved moments of silence, even for students in a public school, moments of silence would also be permissible at the start of a school board meeting, whether or not students were in attendance.

Santa Fe Indep. Sch. Dist. v. Doe, 120 S.Ct. 2266 (2000).

The Supreme Court found that prayers conducted before football games were unconstitutional. The Court was particularly concerned that two practices were permitted by an official school district policy: (1) encouraging the students to elect one of their number to pray; and (2) permitting the praying student to use the school public address system to give the prayer at the game. The Court determined that the prayers were not truly student-initiated, but instead were a state endorsement of religion.

Chief Justice Rehnquist and Justice Thomas wrote a dissent in which they lamented the anti-religious tone of the Court's majority decision in this case, a tone that went far beyond the prayer issue and decried all public expression of religion. The dissent also pointed out that the tone of the decision was not faithful to the Establishment Clause and that President George Washington himself had proclaimed days of fasting and public prayer for the nation. This decision is a reminder of how far America has moved from its Judeo-Christian heritage. The dissent decried the hostility of the majority opinion.

> The Court distorts existing precedent to conclude that the school district's student-message program is invalid on its face under the Establishment Clause. But even more disturbing than its holding is the tone of the Court's opinion: it bristles with hostility to all things religious in public life.

Following this decision many sports fans and team members expressed their disapproval of this decision and continued to exercise their right to spontaneous prayer, without school endorsement. Some Christian fans decided to remain standing after the national anthem and recite the Lord's Prayer in unison in order to honor God before the game. Since such spontaneous prayer by the fans does not involve any action by school officials or use of the school's public address system, this activity is constitutional. Some football team members also decided on their own to gather mid-field for a team prayer. As long as no coaches or other school officials are involved and the prayer is voluntary and student-initiated, it is constitutionally protected student speech.

Chandler v. James, 180 F.3d 1254 (11th Cir. 1999), reinstated by 230 F.3d 1313 (11th Cir. 2000).

An Alabama statute permitting nonsectarian, non-proselytizing, student-initiated prayers at school-related events was held to be unconstitutional. However, the court also held that an injunction prohibiting schools from allowing any student-initiated speech was also unconstitutional. Schools are required to permit student prayer that is truly student-initiated. A court may only enjoin teachers and school officials from commanding, endorsing, or participating in student prayer or religious speech.

Sioux Falls School District Religion Policy

This Sioux Falls School District religion policy was approved by the ***Eighth Circuit Court of Appeals in Florey v. Sioux Falls School District***, 619 F.2d 1311 (8th Cir.), *cert. denied*, 449 U.S. 987 (1980).)

I. POLICY

Recognition of Religious Beliefs and Customs

It is accepted that no religious belief or nonbelief should be promoted by the school district or its employees, and none should be disparaged. Instead, the school district should encourage all students and staff members to appreciate and be tolerant of each other's religious views. The school district should utilize its opportunity to foster understanding and mutual respect among students and parents, whether it involves race, culture, economic background or religious beliefs. In that spirit of tolerance, students and staff members should be excused from participating in practices which are contrary to their religious beliefs unless there are clear issues of overriding concern that would prevent it.

The Sioux Falls School District recognizes that one of its educational goals is to advance the students' knowledge and appreciation of the role that our religious heritage has played in the social, cultural and historical development of civilization.

II. RULES

Observance of Religious Holidays

The practice of the Sioux Falls School District shall be as follows:

1. The several holidays throughout the year which have a religious and a secular basis may be observed in the public schools.
2. The historical and contemporary values and the origin of

religious holidays may be explained in an unbiased and objective manner without sectarian indoctrination.

3. Music, art, literature and drama having religious themes or basis are permitted as part of the curriculum for school-sponsored activities and programs if presented in a prudent and objective manner and as a traditional part of the cultural and religious heritage of the particular holiday.

4. The use of religious symbols such as a cross, menorah, crescent, Star of David, crèche, symbols of Native American religions or other symbols that are a part of a religious holiday is permitted as a teaching aid or resource provided such symbols are displayed as an example of the cultural and religious heritage of the holiday and are temporary in nature. Among these holidays are included Christmas, Easter, Passover, Hanukkah, St. Valentine's Day, St. Patrick's Day, Thanksgiving and Halloween.

5. The school district's calendar should be prepared so as to minimize conflicts with religious holidays of all faiths.

Religion in the Curriculum

Religious institutions and orientations are central to human experience, past and present. An education excluding such a significant aspect would be incomplete. It is essential that the teaching about and not of religion be conducted in a factual objective and respectful manner.

Therefore, the practice of the Sioux Falls School District shall be as follows:

1. The District supports the inclusion of religious literature, music, drama and the arts in the curriculum and in school activities provided it is intrinsic to the learning experience in the various fields of study and is presented objectively.

2. The emphasis on religious themes in the arts, literature and history should be only as extensive as necessary for a balanced and comprehensive study of these areas. Such studies should never foster any particular religious tenet or demean any religious beliefs.

3. Student-initiated expressions to questions or assignments which reflect their beliefs or nonbeliefs about a religious theme shall be accommodated. For example, students are free to express religious belief or nonbelief in compositions, art forms, music, speech and debate.

Dedications and Commencement

Traditions are a cherished part of the community life and the Sioux Falls School District expresses an interest in maintaining those traditions which have had a significance to the community. Such ceremonies should recognize the religious pluralism of the community. Therefore, the practice of the Sioux Falls School District shall be as follows:

1. A dedication ceremony should recognize the religious pluralism of the community and be appropriate to those who use the facility. An open invitation should be extended to all citizens to participate in the ceremony.

2. Traditions, i. e., invocation and benediction, inherent in commencement ceremonies, should be honored in the spirit of accommodation and good taste.

3. Because the baccalaureate service is traditionally religious in nature, it should be sponsored by agencies separate from the Sioux Falls School District.

Duval County Graduation Message Guidelines

(These guidelines were declared constitutional by the Eleventh Circuit Federal Court of Appeals in 2001.)

The purpose of these guidelines is to allow students to direct their own graduation message without monitoring or review by school officials.

1. The use of a brief opening and/or closing message, not to exceed two minutes, at high school graduation exercises shall rest within the discretion of the graduating senior class.
2. The opening and/or closing message shall be given by a student volunteer, in the graduating senior class, chosen by the graduating senior class as a whole.
3. If the graduating senior class chooses to use an opening and/or closing message, the content of that message shall be prepared by the student volunteer and shall not be monitored or otherwise reviewed by Duval County School Board, its officers or employees.

CONCERNING OUTSIDE COMMUNITY VOLUNTEERS

Four major avenues exist for outside (non-school) community volunteers to provide ministry for students in public schools:

1. Off campus support for leaders of student initiated/ student led Equal Access Bible Clubs.
2. A released time program sponsored and led by outside volunteers.
3. An after-school program sponsored and led by an outside group.
4. Conducting community-led baccalaureate services for graduating students, where religious expression is appropriate, even if the service is conducted on school premises.

Equal Access Bible Clubs

Equal Access Bible Clubs are legally protected religious clubs as long as they are initiated and led by the students. Outside religious leaders who want to help with the club should work with student leaders outside of school and away from the school campus to assist these club leaders to learn to minister effectively to their peers. The Equal Access Act does not permit outside speakers to attend the club regularly, but only to visit as special speakers on an occasional basis (generally about once a month and not always the same person). When outside religious leaders are invited by the students to speak to the club, their message may be entirely religious.

Released Time Programs

Released time programs have been around for over half a century and were held to be constitutional in the 1950s. However, they are sometimes ignored because they require a great deal of volunteer commitment and convenient meeting space outside the school building. In a released time program, the school board approves children to be taken from the school to another location, such as a church or private college, where non-school volunteers provide Bible lessons for the students. Released time programs peaked in 1947 with 2 million students enrolled in 2,200 community-sponsored programs. Currently, it is estimated that there are over 1,000 released time programs involving over 250,000 students in kindergarten through high school.

After School Clubs

An outside organization is permitted to conduct after school clubs for students at school facilities on the same basis as other groups are permitted to use the facilities after school for non-school sponsored events and activities. Every school has a "school-use" policy, which the outside group must follow in order to obtain use of school space for an after school religious club. The school may not treat a religious club differently from a secular club.

Baccalaureate Services

A church, a group of churches or other community organization may sponsor a Baccalaureate Service for graduating students---whether graduating from Kindergarten, middle school or high school. This Service is a much overlooked means of bringing the Gospel to students since it may be entirely religious in nature. The sponsors may distribute Bibles to students, engage in prayer and bring an inspirational message of a religious nature to students. Sponsors may conduct the service at a church or other community location, or they may rent or use school facilities on the same basis as other outside groups, based on the school's "use policy." Attendance at the service must be voluntary. Teachers and school officials may voluntarily attend the Service, but they may not officially participate in the religious program.

Baccalaureate Services were once a common and accepted part of graduation exercises. Prior to the 1960s, the Baccalaureate Service was sponsored by the school, generally on the Sunday evening prior to the Graduation Ceremony itself. It was a time for religious and inspirational messages for the students. A comeback of the Baccalaureate Service, now sponsored by private community groups or churches, seems long overdue. Instead of a diploma, students could be presented with personally inscribed Bibles or other religious items. School officials may have no part in the planning or carrying out of a Baccalaureate Service except to voluntarily attend as private citizens.

The following questions are those that are most often asked about religious outreach to public schools by non-school individuals and groups.

What may religious volunteers do to assist an Equal Access Bible Club?

The federal Equal Access Act requires that public schools permit student-initiated and student-led Bible Clubs to meet in school on the same basis as other non-curricular clubs are permitted to meet. While a teacher may be assigned to the club as a monitor, the teacher may not participate in any substantive religious activities with the students. Similarly, under the provisions of the Equal Access Act, an outside volunteer, such as a community youth pastor, is not permitted to meet regularly with the students or to lead the club for them.

Outside religious leaders may work with the club's student leaders away from the school campus and on non-school time to help them learn to minister effectively to their peers. Even a teacher, volunteering outside school time and away from the school, could assist the club's student leaders in this manner. The Equal Access Act, passed by Congress in 1984, does not permit outside speakers to attend the club regularly, but only on an occasional basis (probably no more than once a month and not always the same person).

The Equal Access Bible Club must be student-led. However, many pastors and others who work with student leaders away from the school have been encouraged by how elementary and middle school students, as well as high school students, rise to the occasion and become great soul winners and Bible teachers for their peers.

What is a Released Time program?

More than a half century ago, the Supreme Court held that public schools may adjust their schedules to accommodate the spiritual needs of students through participation in released time programs. A released time program is implemented when students (with the written permission of their parents) are excused from attendance for a part of the school day to attend hour-long sectarian religious classes at churches, synagogues, or other facilities away from the school campus.

Often churches or other institutions, such as local Bible colleges, combine their resources to run the program. If the program is ecumenical, parents may choose which of several classes they wish their children to attend. Or a single church or local Bible college may sponsor the program for all students who wish to participate.

> *The released time program must be taught by community volunteers and must take place away from the school campus.*

Subject to applicable state laws, schools have the discretion to dismiss their students for these off-campus religious classes. School personnel may neither encourage nor discourage participation by the students. Neither the students who attend nor those who remain at school may be penalized for their decision. During the class period in which the released time program is conducted (often the last period of the day or before lunch), the students who do not attend may be given a study hall or some other non-curricular activity.

Schools may not permit such sectarian religious instruction to take place on the school campus. Nor may school personnel be used to teach such sectarian religious classes. The released time program must be taught by community volunteers and must take place away from the school campus.

How may churches or other community sponsors implement a Released Time program?

Released time is the most under-used method by which outside groups can reach public school children for Christ. One reason that released time programs are so underused is that they can be difficult to coordinate and they require a large number of volunteers.

> *Released time is the most under-used method by which outside groups can reach public school children for Christ.*

Schools boards must provide authorization for released time programs and should be requested to do so by the parents, students, and sponsors. Various courts have set the following standards for released time programs.

- School officials must permit notice of released time programs in the same way as community-sponsored little league or scouting events are announced. (Generally, the school board will distribute initial information about the program to all parents along with registration blanks and permission slips);
- Parents, churches, or other outside groups may conduct released time programs for public school students;
- Public school authorities must remain neutral with regard to the program;
- Students must be released for religious instruction upon the written request of the parent or guardian;
- Programs must be voluntary; no student may be coerced into attendance;
- Teachers and school personnel may not comment on attendance or non-attendance;
- Students may invite classmates to attend;
- Programs must not be conducted on school property;
- All students must be released at one time;
- Public school students may leave the school for no more than one hour per week to attend religious instruction offered by churches or other religious institutions;

- The religious instruction must be given by non-school personnel;
- The church or other religious body sponsoring the program must make weekly attendance reports to the school and must completely control the program;
- State officials may not monitor or judge the religious message;
- All costs and liability must be borne by the religious group(s) providing the program;
- The sponsoring religious group(s) must assume full responsibility for the students during this off campus time;
- Classroom learning activities in the public school must come to a halt during this released time hour; and
- The hour may be used by the schools for other clubs or study halls for those students not attending the released time program.

How may parents, students and/or community sponsors obtain permission from the school board to establish a released time program?

In order to establish a released time program, parents must first request permission from the local school board. Before approaching the school board, parents and sponsoring religious organizations should have a well-developed plan with specific information about who will teach the program, how students will be transported to the off-site locations where the Bible instruction will take place, and how liability requirements and other costs will be met.

When the plans are completed, the group should schedule a specific time to present their request to the school board. Four or five articulate parents, students, or other sponsors should be selected to testify to the need for and interest in a religious program. The people who are going to present the request will generally need to register ahead of time to speak. They may do so by calling the school administration office before the meeting. School board agendas normally include an open agenda time when citizens can address the board.

Citizens who address the school board are sometimes granted only two or three minutes each to speak (unless the board has questions that extend the time), so the group should plan their presentation well. Printed material explaining the released time program and how it would work should also be distributed to school board members, the press, and the public.

The sponsors may need to be persistent. Depending upon the attitude of school board members and their interest in the program, several approaches may be needed. It may even require the election of new school board members favorable to the project to have the program approved. Petitioners should be sure to inform the local newspapers about the project in order to build community support and interest. Each local paper usually has an education reporter present at school board meetings.

As much as possible, the parents and sponsors who request the released time program should work closely with school board members in developing the concept. Since the school board is a politically elected body, the number of citizens who support the released time program will often influence board members regarding support or non-support for the project. The sponsors should attempt to collect petitions and to have as many supporters attend the school board meeting as possible when the request is made. It is also helpful to have a large number of students who support the program in attendance. The more support shown by the community and students, the more likely the school board will be to approve the idea.

Who determines what is taught in the released time program?

The individual churches or community sponsors determine how the program will be organized and what material will be taught.

Sometimes several churches work together, while other times the program is sponsored by a single community church or by some other community group such as a Bible college or children's evangelism group. In any case, after the program is approved and notices have been sent out and permission slips returned, the school has no further participation in determining how the program will be run. Such decisions are left completely to the sponsoring organizations. The sponsors determine what religious materials will be used, who the teachers will be, where the program will be held, how the children will be transported, and what special promotions, activities, or events will be included.

The released time sponsors are permitted to have either paid personnel or volunteers to teach these released time programs. Sometimes churches will pay Bible college students to teach the program. Given the scope and cost of such a venture, the sponsoring groups must be particularly creative in their approach to providing funding, facilities, and personnel. When properly planned and carried out, these programs can be immensely successful.

May outside groups sponsor after-school Bible clubs for students on school property?

Religious community groups must be given equal access on the same basis as other community groups to use school facilities after school for student club meetings led by outside religious leaders. Teachers should not be involved in encouraging or conducting such meetings; however, courts have permitted teachers to participate in an after school program away from their own school. Schools may distribute information to students about the meetings on the same basis as other information about student community groups or after-school activities is given to students.

May churches rent school facilities for worship services?

Schools are required to treat secular and religious groups alike for purposes of facility use. A school should not allow use of its facilities, including its auditorium, by outside secular groups and then deny equal access to religious groups because they intend to engage in religious worship. Such a denial would be religious discrimination. A school may not prohibit worship or other religious activities in school facilities while permitting secular activities. When school facilities are available for use by the community, the school may not exclude religious groups merely because they are religious.

The church or religious group should request a copy of the "Use Policy" for the school and should be ready to comply with the neutral requirements for use. Some schools may charge a rental or janitorial fee.

Schools are required to treat secular and religious groups alike for purposes of facility use.

The school may not require only a church to be in a building program or to be actively seeking another location before being permitted to regularly use the school facilities. However, if there is a general rule limiting regular use by all organizations or if the school only permits one-time use for special events for all organizations, the church must abide by such fair and neutral policies.

Where may outside sponsors conduct baccalaureate services?

School officials may not mandate or organize religious baccalaureate ceremonies. School officials should have no involvement in private baccalaureate services.

If a school generally opens its facilities to private groups, it must make those facilities available on the same terms to community or religious organizers of privately sponsored religious baccalaureate services. A school may not extend preferential treatment to outside groups sponsoring baccalaureate ceremonies and may, in some instances, be obliged to disclaim official endorsement of such ceremonies.

If a religious group intends to rent a school building for an activity that closely resembles an official school function, such as a baccalaureate service for graduating seniors and their families, it is critical that the school be totally disassociated from planning, promoting, or participating in the event. School employees are permitted to attend, but may participate in such services only in their personal capacities. Baccalaureate services may be held in churches, schools or other facilities.

May Gideons distribute Bibles in public schools?

The Gideons have had a long tradition of coming onto school campuses to distribute Bibles to students. Although students clearly have a right to distribute Bibles to other students, the Gideons, as school outsiders, no longer have the same rights they once had to interact with students. Courts in various jurisdictions have reached various conclusions regarding the distribution of Gideon Bibles in public schools; however, a consensus regarding how this activity may continue appears to be evolving.

Generally, courts look at several factors in deciding whether the Bibles may be distributed:

1. The Gideons may not be excluded simply because their message is religious when the school allows other outside organizations to come on the school campus to distribute information to students.

2. Courts do not permit the Gideons to distribute their Bibles in school classrooms. It is generally required that the Bibles be placed on a table in the hallway where students may choose to pick them up.

3. The timing of the distribution may be considered. Generally, it is better for the Bibles to be made available outside of the classroom just before or just after school.

4. The age of the students may also be a consideration. Generally, courts will look more favorably upon Bible distribution to middle and high school students, rather than to those in the elementary grades.

Of course, the Gideons may also distribute their Bibles on public sidewalks that abut school property. These sidewalks are public forum areas open for free speech, which includes literature distribution.

May soul winners distribute tracts and talk to students on sidewalks that abut school property?

Soul winners are often surprised to learn they can witness to public school students on public sidewalk areas that abut school property. It is always important to determine exactly where public property ends and school property begins to avoid being arrested for trespassing. Some schools have internal sidewalks leading to bus loading areas that appear to be public, but are not.

Soul winners may not be prevented from witnessing or distributing tracts on public sidewalks outside schools, as long as the free speech activity remains orderly, the noise level does not exceed appropriate limits, and there is no interference with the educational activity of the school. However, the soulwinners may be required to remain in a designated area out of the traffic flow.

> *Soul winners are often surprised to learn they can witness to public school students on public sidewalk areas that abut school property.*

Sidewalks abutting school property provide an excellent setting for reaching students because student traffic on the sidewalks is heavy and the government's ability to regulate free speech activity on such public sidewalks is slight. Therefore, groups like the Gideons may not be prevented from handing out Bibles to public school students on public sidewalks abutting school property and other soulwinners may distribute tracts or otherwise interact with students.

Some pro-life groups have also displayed pictures of unborn babies and other pro-life posters on the public sidewalks in front of schools where teenage girls can be influenced before they become pregnant and consider abortion. Sidewalk counselors may also distribute tracts offering help to pregnant girls in these public sidewalk locations.

Unlike public sidewalks that surround and abut school property, the public school parking lot is not a public forum area. Instead, it is considered private property much like the parking lots of stores and shopping malls where soul winners are required to have permission to witness..

Soul winners, Gideons, or pro-life counselors might want to consider notifying school officials that they will be exercising their free speech rights on the sidewalks abutting school property. Otherwise, school officials might wonder what is going on and assume that the activities are illegal (i.e., drug-related) or nefarious.

May pastors visit with students during lunch periods?

Public school officials have discretion to control who is permitted entry to school facilities during the school day. Generally, outside visitors must sign in at the office or otherwise announce their presence at the school. This is a safety measure for students.

Sometimes a school limits such entry to parents or guardians of the children. Sometimes no outsiders are permitted in the school or in the lunchroom. However, if a school principal determines to open the facilities for outside visitors to interact with students or to join them in the lunchroom, pastors may not be excluded merely because of their religious viewpoint.

When a pastor visits a student for lunch or for any other purpose, the pastor should remain with that student and with any friends of the student who voluntary approach or sit down to eat. The pastor should not generally roam about the lunchroom or hallways and interact with all students, unless permitted to do so by the principal or other school official. However, since permission for such activities is discretionary with school officials, pastors may do as much visitation with students as school officials permit.

May public school counseling programs include pastors?

A public school counselor may offer counseling programs to students with a spiritual component if the overall program addresses secular problems and the counselor does not coerce a student's attendance. For instance, a school counselor may suggest assistance programs, such as Alcoholics Anonymous, that have a spiritual component. Schools may also provide students with a choice of counselors, including religious counselors.

A school counselor may involve a pastor or other persons with a religious perspective as part of a larger secular and neutral mentoring program for students who are seeking such spiritual assistance. However, the counselor must make a variety of options available to the student—both secular and religious—and there should be no coercion for a student to choose a religious program. For example, the school counselor should not give a student a choice between detention or AA. The counselor should also consider and be respectful of each family's religious or non-religious background when offering assistance to the student.

A mentoring program that used only clergy volunteers as mentors was declared to be unconstitutional, but the court indicated that clergy volunteers could participate in a larger secular program that also included non-clergy mentors. The same would be true for tutors. Many churches participate in school tutoring programs where church members offer their services to students. As long as students have a choice between religious or non-religious tutors or mentors, this arrangement is generally permissible.

School counselors have a great deal of discretion regarding which outside persons to include in mentoring or tutoring programs with the students. Pastors or others who want to participate in such programs should get to know the school counselor and offer their services directly as part of a larger secular program.

May a school distribute notices in class for outside religious activities available to students?

As discussed more fully in the question regarding distribution of notices for released time programs, it is permissible for schools to distribute literature to students in the classroom notifying them of various community group activities, such as Little League.

Religious notices should not be excluded merely because they are religious. However, religious groups who want to distribute notices of, for instance, a basketball clinic to be held at a church, should include only the date, time, place, sponsoring organization and activity. No Bible verses or proselytizing material should be included on the notice except that the sponsor or activity description should give enough notice to the students and parents that the activity is religious.

Cases Controlling Released Time Programs

Zorach v. Clauson, 343 U.S. 306 (1952).

The United States Supreme Court has upheld the constitutionality of released time programs in which participating children go to religious classes held away from the public school. Released time programs are constitutional if they are voluntary and are not sponsored by the school. In writing for the majority of the Court, Justice William O. Douglas said:

> We are a religious people whose institutions presuppose a Supreme Being. When the State encourages religious instruction or cooperates with religious authorities by adjusting the schedule of public events to sectarian needs, it then follows the best of our traditions, for it then respects the religious nature of our people and accommodates the public services to their spiritual needs. To hold that it may not would be to find in the Constitution a requirement that the government show a callous indifference to religious groups. That would be preferring those who believe in no religion over those who do believe. We find no constitutional requirement which makes it necessary for government to be hostile to religion and to throw its weight against efforts to widen the effective scope of religious influence.

Smith v. Smith, 523 F.2d 121 (4th Cir. 1975), cert. denied, 423 U.S. 1073 (1976).

The court approved the practice of providing school enrollment lists to sponsors of released time programs even for elementary age students. The sponsoring group then uses the student enrollment list obtained from the school to mail information and consent forms directly to parents. If the public school wants the released time program to use a particular consent form, the court held that it was permissible for the school to provide a sample form for use by the released time sponsor. After the parents fill out the parental consent form, the court held that the children are permitted to return the signed forms directly to the school.

Lanner v. Wimmer, 662 F.2d. 1349 (10th Cir. 1981).

Released time instruction must be given by non-school personnel away from the school campus. The court considered it to be minimal involvement by the school to assist with the registration and record-keeping aspects of the program. However, the court did not permit the school to assume the task of regular attendance keeping for the program after the registration and parental permission slip process was concluded and the students had returned their registration and permission slips to the school. The cost of printing and maintaining attendance cards is the responsibility of the sponsoring organization, which then makes weekly attendance reports to the school. The court held:

> The registration and record keeping involved are necessary to administer the released-time program and do not excessively entangle the government in religion or indicate the school's endorsement of the content of released-time courses. The integration of the released-time program into the public school schedule is nothing more than an administrative effort to accommodate the released-time program with as little inconvenience to students as possible.

Doe v. Shenandoah County Sch. Bd., 737 F. Supp. 913 (W.D. Va. 1990).

Portable instruction sites may not be located on school campuses for conducting released time programs and no academic credit may be given.

Doe v. Porter, 188 F. Supp.2d 904 (E.D. Tenn. 2002).

Religious groups may not teach unmonitored, sectarian religion courses on school premises during the school day. Here, the court found that the courses were not truly elective because the alternative was for the students to repeat another class in place of the religious class.

Pierce ex rel. Pierce v. Sullivan West Central School Dist., 379 F.3d 56 (2nd Cir. 2004).

In a decision similar to *Zorach* the court stated that released time programs as they are used in New York do not violate the Establishment Clause

Cases Controlling the Use of Public Schools by Outside Groups

Gregoire v. Centennial Sch. Dist., 907 F.2d 1366, 1370 (3rd Cir. 1990).

Generally speaking, a school district is under no obligation to open its facilities to expressive activity by outsiders, but if a school is open for such purposes, it must be open to everyone, including religious groups, in the same manner.

Planned Parenthood of Southern Nevada, Inc. v. Clark County School Dist., 941 F.2d 817 (9th Cir. 1991).

A school newspaper is not a traditional open forum, nor did the school intend to open it as a forum, so the school could refuse to print advertisements for a family planning organization.

Lamb's Chapel v. Center Moriches Union Free Sch. Dist., 508 U.S. 384 (1993).

If a public school or university allows public or private organizations to rent school property for meetings when school is not in session, the school cannot deny religious organizations use of the property merely because subjects will be discussed from a religious viewpoint.

Good News/Good Sports Club v. School District of Ladue, 28 F.3d 1501 (8th Cir. 1994).

A parent-led, community-based Christian club was permitted to meet on the premises of a junior high school immediately after school hours because a Boy Scout group, which was also concerned with the moral development of young people, was also permitted to meet there.

Good News Club v. Milford Central School District, 121 S.Ct. 2093 (2001).

The Supreme Court held that it was unconstitutional viewpoint discrimination in violation of the Free Speech Clause for a public school to exclude a Christian children's club from meeting after hours on school property merely because of the religious viewpoint of the club. The school had already opened its facilities for secular after-school activities "pertaining to the welfare of the community," and could not discriminate against the group because it discussed "the development of character and morals from a religious perspective." The school had excluded the club because its activities included learning Bible verses, relating Bible stories to the children's lives, and prayer. Merely because the club's activities were "decidedly religious in nature" did not mean that their activities could not also be characterized properly as the teaching of morals and character development from a particular viewpoint. The school was not required to engage in viewpoint discrimination in order to avoid violating the Establishment Clause. The Court once again affirmed the fundamental proposition of constitutional law that a governmental body may not suppress or exclude the speech of private parties for the sole reason that the speech is religious or contains a religious perspective.

Cases Controlling Private Baccalaureate Services

Miller v. Cooper, 224 P.2d 520 (N.M. 1952).

A baccalaureate service could be held in a church where there were no other suitable auditorium facilities available. In 1952, public schools were still officially sponsoring the baccalaureate services. Today, private baccalaureate services may be held in a church or at the school, using normal policies for outside use of school facilities.

Verbena United Methodist Church v. Chilton County Bd. of Educ., 765 F. Supp. 704 (M.D. Ala, 1991).

Where a school board has created a public forum by allowing use of its auditorium and other similar public school facilities by a broad range of community organizations on an essentially unrestricted basis and for a wide variety of expressive activities, including charity fund raisers, social gatherings, and events of a religious nature, the school board must permit a church to rent the high school auditorium to conduct an unofficial "baccalaureate service". It was not incompatible with the Establishment Clause for the board to permit a baccalaureate service organized and presided over by church pastors or other community religious leaders, despite the inclusion of speeches, prayer, and songs with a Christian theme, as long as the board (1) took steps to disclaim any official connection to the event and (2) ensured that no school officials promoted, led, or participated in the service.

Randall v. Pegan, 765 F. Supp. 793 (W.D. N.Y. 1991).

It does not violate the Establishment Clause for a school to lease facilities to a student religious group for a baccalaureate service. The school did not plan or endorse the service.

Shumway v. Albany County Sch. Dist., 826 F. Supp. 1320 (D. Wyo. 1993).

A school district was required to permit a student religious group access to school facilities for a baccalaureate service.

Goodwin v. Cross County Schools, 394 F. Supp. 417 (E.D. Ark. 1971).

Gideons were not permitted to distribute Bibles to school children in elementary classrooms. Along with the Bible distribution, the Gideon representative in this case had also given illustrated talks to the children about the Bible.

Berger v. Rensselaer Cent School Corp., 982 F.2d 1160 (7th Cir. 1993).

Gideon's distribution of Bibles in fifth grade classrooms was held to violate the Establishment Clause of the First Amendment.

Peck v. Upshur County Bd. of Educ., 155 F.3d 274 (4th Cir. 1998).

Religious groups such as the Gideons are permitted to distribute literature (including Bibles) to students in public school buildings during the school day if school officials permit other groups such as the Little League, the 4-H Club, the Boy Scouts, and the Women's Christian Temperance Union to distribute informational pamphlets to students during the school day. However, the Bibles could not be distributed in the classroom, but were required to be placed on a table in the hallway where students could choose to take one.

The court held that a school must provide equal access for all outside groups alike, whether secular or religious. Therefore, if the school permits outside secular groups to distribute notices of activities for students, "discrimination against religious speech in such a forum could violate the First Amendment." The court went on to explain that the school board does "nothing more than affirm the right of religious speakers to use the [school] forums on equal terms with others, . . . and the Supreme Court has explicitly held that preventing discrimination against religious and other types of speech in a school forum is an undeniably secular purpose." The court held:

> [Where] there is a sufficiently vigorous exchange of informational announcements and pamphlets . . . the schools could

allow distribution of religious materials of a "similar" character, but also that the schools would risk unconstitutionally discriminating against religious speech were they to exclude such religious materials . . . [T]he schools could encounter constitutional difficulties if they refused to distribute 're-ligious' materials that were analogous to informational announcements by the scouts, 4-H, or the Little League.

Child Evangelism Fellowship of Md., Inc. v. Montgomery County Public Schools, 368 F.Supp.2d 416 (D.Md. 2005).

School mailbox distribution system is not a public forum, so the school may limit the topics that are addressed through it. This court ruled that the school could limit access to its inter-school mail system to organizations with "traditional educational relevance," thus barring the Good News Club from distributing its flyer. The court found that the Good News Club had other means of distributing its information and the school's policy was neutral and was not a pretext for viewpoint discrimination. Note cases regarding distribution of notices for religious programs at the end of this section.

Doe v. S. Iron R-1 Sch. Dist., 498 F.3e 878 (8th Cir. 2007).

Gideon representatives were not permitted to distribute Bibles to Fifth Grade students in their classrooms during instructional times.

Cases Controlling Witnessing in Public Forum Areas Around Public Schools

Grayned v. Rockford, 408 U.S. 104 (1972).

Free speech expression may be regulated for noise content in appropriate places, such as schools while classes are in session. The general test is to ask whether the expressive activity is basically incompatible with the normal activities of a particular place at a particular time.

Perry Educ. Ass'n v. Perry Local Educators' Ass'n, 460 U.S. 37 (1983).

Much like a private property owner, school officials have the power to preserve the property under their control for the use to which it is lawfully dedicated. They may not, however, allow discussion on a subject and then discriminate based on viewpoints of that subject.

Grattan v. Bd. of School Comm'r of Baltimore City, 805 F.2d 1160 (4th Cir. 1986).

A public school parking lot is not a public forum for purposes of free speech.

Reed v. State, 762 S.W.2d 640 (Tex.App. 1988).

A man was convicted of criminal trespass when he refused to leave an on-campus sidewalk where he was distributing anti-abortion literature to high school students as they got off school busses. A sidewalk located on school property is not a public forum.

Bacon v. Bradley-Bourbonnais High School Dist., 707 F. Supp. 1005 (C.D. Ill. 1989).

Witnessing and Bible or tract distribution may not be prevented on public sidewalks that abut public school property.

Seidman v. Paradise Valley Unified School Dist. No. 69, 327 F.Supp.2d 1098 (D.Ariz. 2004).

The school Parent Teacher Organization sold customizable tiles to be placed in the school, but prohibited messages such as "God Bless [student's name]." The court stated that it "found no authority allowing viewpoint discrimination when the speech merely bears the imprimatur of the school and the forum is located on school property." The court ruled that the school had to allow the religious message.

Kiesinger v. Mexico Academy and Cent. School, 427 F. Supp. 2d 182 (N.D.N.Y. 2006).

When a school invited members of the community to purchase bricks in a school walkway and specify inscriptions on them, it designated a limited open forum. This means they could proscribe certain topics, but could not allow a topic and then proscribe certain viewpoints on it. For example, the school could not remove bricks referring to Jesus, but leave other bricks referring to God in a more generic way.

Cases Controlling Involvement of Religious Leaders in School Programs

Doe v. Beaumont Indep. Sch. Dist., 240 F.3d 462 (5th Cir. 2001).

The court ruled that a school district program enlisting religious volunteers to counsel students on secular topics violated the Establishment Clause. The court held that in this case the program did not have a secular purpose and it impermissibly endorsed religion. However the court implied that the program could have been approved if the religious volunteers were merely a part of a wider group of counselors that permitted the school to provide counseling choices for students.

Hansen v. Ann Arbor Public Schools, 293 F.Supp.2d 780 (E.D. Mich. 2003).

The student-led Gay/Straight Alliance club organized a panel discussion for "Diversity Week," and only invited pro-homosexual religious leaders to participate. When a Christian student requested that other religious viewpoints be included, the school denied her request. The court ruled that the school district violated the establishment of religion clause by sponsoring a panel composed only of clergy representatives who believed that homosexuality was consistent with religion. The court found no secular purpose, as required by the Supreme Court's *Lemon* Test, and held that the primary effect of the panel was to impermissibly advance a government preferred religious view that homosexuality and religion were compatible. The court also found there was an excessive entanglement with religion by the school district in recruiting clergy panel members having only one particular viewpoint.

Cases Controlling Notice Distribution for Religious Programs

Sherman v. Comm. Sch. Dist., 8 F.3d 1160 (7th Cir. 1993), cert. denied, 511 U.S. 110 (1994).

The court held that distributing notices for community activities does not violate the Establishment Clause, even when the activities are of a religious nature. Legal standards for equal treatment require that all groups be treated alike, whether religious or secular. However, schools may require that no devotional or proselytizing material be included on the notice, but merely the time, place, date, activity, and sponsor information. The Establishment Clause principle of "separation of church and state" was not violated when a school officially distributed information inviting students to an organization where members were required to affirm a religious belief, because the religious notice had been provided in the same manner and on the same basis as information from other non religious community groups.

Hills v. Scottsdale Unified School Dist. No. 48, 329 F.3d 1044 (9th Cir. 2003).

If a school allowed businesses and community programs to distribute literature and fliers about their programs, it could not prohibit a Christian summer camp from doing the same simply because it was Christian.

Child Evangelism Fellowship of New Jersey Inc. v. Stafford Tp. School Dist., 386 F.3d 514 (3rd Cir. 2004).

The school created a limited public forum when it allowed community groups to distribute fliers advertising their programs. Therefore the school could not bar a religious group merely on the basis of the religious nature of the program because similar secular groups were permitted to advertise. Schools may not discriminate on the basis of viewpoint.

Scalise v. Boy Scouts of America, 692 N.W.2d 858 (Mich. App. 2005).

The court rejected a parent's claim that allowing the Boy Scouts to distribute flyers at school and use school facilities after school violated the Establishment Clause because of its requirement that members and leaders recite a theistic oath.

NATIONAL CENTER FOR LIFE AND LIBERTY

Center for Life Defense: Dallas, TX

The Center for Life Defense protects and defends the lives of the elderly, disabled, and unborn, speaking for those who cannot speak for themselves in courtrooms, hospitals, and legislatures.

Center to Advance the USA: Washington, D.C.

The Center to Advance the USA provides model legislation and actively meets with state and federal elected officials to promote Biblical values in government and to educate legislators and citizens to stand for God-honoring principles. AdvanceUSA Ambassadors pray, network, educate, and inform their members of Congress on life and liberty issues.

Center for Church Liberty: Washington, D.C.

The Center for Church Liberty ensures that all our affiliated pastors and churches are legally protected and empowered to reach their communities for Jesus Christ.

Center for Christian Education: Tampa, FL

The Center for Christian Education legally serves, protects, and empowers our partner schools to teach and train this generation for Christ.

Center for Homeschool Liberty: Tampa, FL

The Center for Homeschool Liberty protects the right of parents to educate their children at home in accordance with their Biblical values and worldview.

The NCLL litigates cases, advances legislation, and speaks to the culture to advance life and liberty for all Americans.

Our legal team is committed to this guiding principle:

"If it's wrong, fight it; if it's right, fight for it."

To learn more visit us at
www.NCLL.org
http://www.facebook.com/thencll
http://twitter.com/yourNCLL

14668582R00124

Made in the USA
San Bernardino, CA
01 September 2014